World's Worst AIRCRAFT

Jim Winchester

ROSEN
PUBLISHING®

New York

This edition first published in 2009 by:

The Rosen Publishing Group, Inc.

29 E. 21st Street

New York, NY 10010

Project Editor: James Bennett

Picture Research: James Hollingworth

Design: EQ Media

Library of Congress Cataloging-in-Publication Data

Winchester, Jim.

World's worst aircraft / Jim Winchester.

 p. cm.—(World's worst : from innovation to disaster)

Includes index.

ISBN-13: 978-1-4042-1837-6 (library binding)

1. Airplanes—History—Juvenile literature. 2. System failures (Engineering)—Juvenile literature. I. Title.

TL547.W653 2009

629.133'3—dc22

                                        2008011532

Manufactured in the United States of America

Photo Credits: All images courtesy Aerospace/Art-Tech except: Cody Images: 14, 36, 66; Philip Jarrett: 20, 40

On the cover: the British Rolls-Royce "Flying Bedstead" of 1954

CONTENTS

INTRODUCTION

The choice of the "worst" aircraft contained in this volume is the author's own, although friends offered many suggestions. As such it should not be regarded as definitive in any way. Strictly speaking, a number of these entries could be considered more as "flops" than "worst" in the sense of having many inherent faults.

Most of the aircraft here have some redeeming features. Many were arguably not bad at all. Some were commercially unsuccessful; others no longer met military requirements or followed them too rigidly. Some definitely should never have left the drawing board. One or two barely did – only making it as far as a mock-up or partly completed prototype.

A few manufacturers appear again and again in this book. Generally speaking a few bad aircraft will appear from time to time in any company's stable – if the company keeps going long enough and is willing to try new things. A number of the plane makers featured here are of course still in business. Nothing written here is meant as a slur on these companies and their current products. After all, if they are still making aircraft (and only a handful of the manufacturers mentioned in this book still are) they must be doing something right.

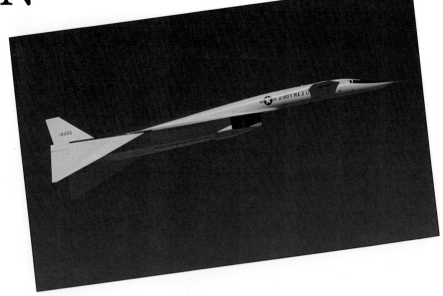

Above: The Mach 3 North American XB-70 was a remarkable technological achievement, but fell victim to changes in the political and military climate, massive complexity, and eye-watering cost.

Above: At the other end of the scale, the Hiller VZ-1 was a man-size contraption that allowed a soldier to hover off the ground making a very loud noise as he did so. No practical use was found for the aircraft.

Until the 1920s, it can be argued that aircraft design was in its infancy and there was still much to learn, so it is perhaps unfair to be too harsh on some of the designs from this era. What seems blindingly obvious as a disaster waiting to happen today must have looked like the next great advance in aeronautics. Nonetheless, plenty of designers fell into the "should have known better" category. Some inventors persisted with attempts to prove that the Wright Brothers, Louis Blériot and other great pioneers had it all wrong, and built multiplanes, ornithopters and other devices that largely vibrated themselves to bits before putting their pilots in too much danger, but, at least, not from a high fall.

Fewer aircraft that qualify as "bad" are made these days. Extensive computer modeling and simulation allows the bugs to be ironed out before metal (or carbon fiber) is cut. The small number of major aircraft projects and their great cost make aerospace companies somewhat risk averse, as failure can easily "cost the farm."

All the aircraft contained in here were somebody's labor of love and all represent someone's dream, costing a lot of money and effort in their day. A number saw the wasting of large fortunes, the careers of many talented people, and the lives of their crews. It is easy to take cheap shots at someone who has tried and failed, but the author (who has not designed any flying machines to date) hopes he has been able to find the humor in some of these stories of aircraft that never quite took off.

BAD TIMING

Most of the aircraft in this section could have been great successes, but appeared too late and were immediately obsolescent, or conversely were initially successful but past their sell-by date when most needed. Some of these embodied notable firsts, but either the times changed or they didn't.

Unfortunately for military aircraft the consequence of obsolescence has usually been measured in young men's lives. Failed combat aircraft were usually shunted to training or second-line units as soon as possible, but in many cases not before they had suffered heavy attrition, as with the Douglas TBD and the Fairey Battle.

Military requirements move on, particularly in wartime. The Boeing Sea Ranger was obsolete by the time it was built, but only because the US Navy had changed its strategy following the opening battles of the Pacific War. The Douglas Mixmaster would have been marvelous if it had appeared a year or two earlier than it did. Conversely, the proposed attack variant would have been useful in Korea if the USAF had persisted with it.

In the civil field, the attempt to produce a replacement for the DC-3 led to many false starts, including the Saab Scandia and the Aviation Traders Accountant.

Left: The giant Bristol Brabazon. Building an airliner larger than a 747 proved beyond the resources of Britain's postwar aircraft industry.

DOUGLAS TBD DEVASTATOR *(1935)*

The TBD Devastator was the US Navy's first monoplane torpedo-bomber and embodied many new features. Combat tactics changed little from the biplane era, however. An effective torpedo attack requires a slow and steady approach, making the Devastators easy targets. Once the TBD had braved fighters and ships' guns of all calibers, the success of its attack depended on whether the torpedo ran true and if it actually exploded against the target. US wartime torpedoes were notoriously ineffective. Although Devastators sank one Japanese carrier at Coral Sea, the Battle of Midway in June 1942 saw the TBD force wiped out without inflicting damage on the Japanese.

Only five of the 41 TBDs involved in the battle made it back and the battle left fewer than 20 TBDs in the inventory. By August 1942 they were withdrawn from the front line.

SPECIFICATIONS

CREW:	3
ENGINE:	one 671kW (900hp) Pratt & Whitney R-1830-64 Twin Wasp radial piston engine
MAX SPEED:	208mph (332km/h)
SPAN:	50ft (15.24m)
LENGTH:	35ft (10.67m)
HEIGHT:	15ft 1in (4.60m)
WEIGHT:	maximum 10,194lb (4624kg)

Left: At the Battle of Midway the lumbering Devastator's main achievement was to distract the Japanese from the dive-bomber attacks. The cost included an entire Devastator squadron and all but one of its aviators.

For the first time in a Navy bomber the TBD featured an enclosed cockpit and all-metal construction. The corrugated wing surfaces contributed to strength but increased drag.

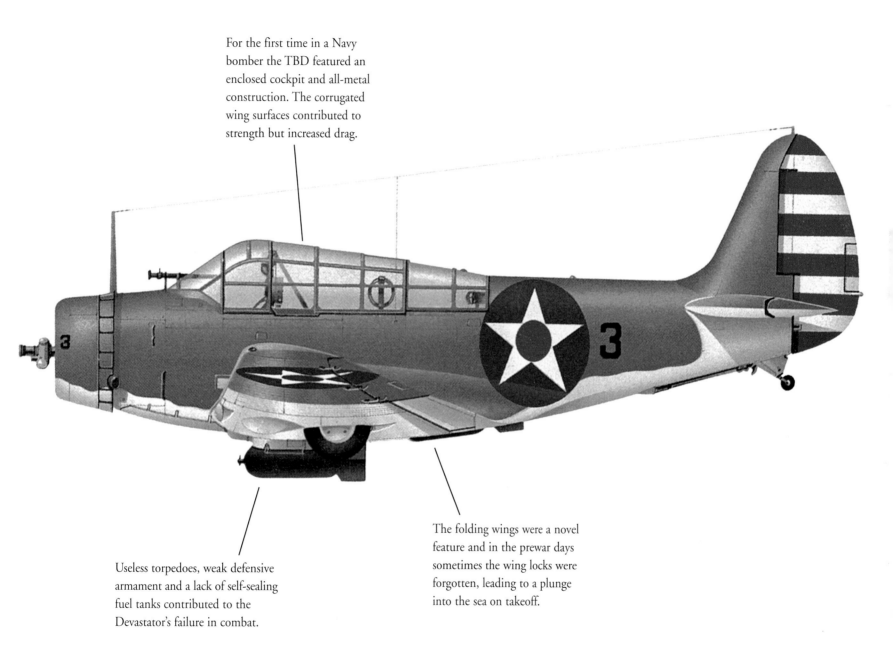

Useless torpedoes, weak defensive armament and a lack of self-sealing fuel tanks contributed to the Devastator's failure in combat.

The folding wings were a novel feature and in the prewar days sometimes the wing locks were forgotten, leading to a plunge into the sea on takeoff.

FAIREY BATTLE *(1936)*

Designed in 1932–33, the Battle, with its metal skin and streamlined monoplane layout, was the height of modernity when it appeared in 1936, but by the outbreak of war was too unmaneuverable and slow to avoid modern fighters and too lightly armed to cause much damage.

On May 10, 1940 the Battles were thrown into action against the German advance into the Low Countries, making low-level raids against convoys, troops and bridges. All attacking aircraft were shot down or damaged on the first day. An attack on bridges over the Albert Canal resulted in total losses and the awarding of two (posthumous) Victoria Crosses. Belgium's small force of Battles was expended in the same attack. Battles were soon relegated to roles such as target tugs and, with a particularly ugly two-cockpit version, training.

SPECIFICATIONS (Mk I)

CREW:	3
ENGINE:	one 1,030hp (768kW) Rolls-Royce Merlin IV-12 piston engine
MAX SPEED:	257mph (414km/h)
SPAN:	54ft (16.46m)
LENGTH:	42ft 4in (12.90m)
HEIGHT:	15ft 6in (4.72m)
WEIGHT:	maximum 10,792lb (4895kg)

Left: Nearly 2,200 Battles were built for the RAF and friendly air forces. After a spectacularly short combat career, they were found uses away from the front line, in places like South Africa and Canada.

The Battle had the same Merlin engine as the Spitfire Mk I, but when loaded weighed nearly half as much again, giving it a top speed over 100mph (160km/h) less than the Spitfire.

The Battle was designed as a two-seater with crew of pilot and observer, but provision was later made for a gunner, armed with a single World War I-vintage Vickers machine gun.

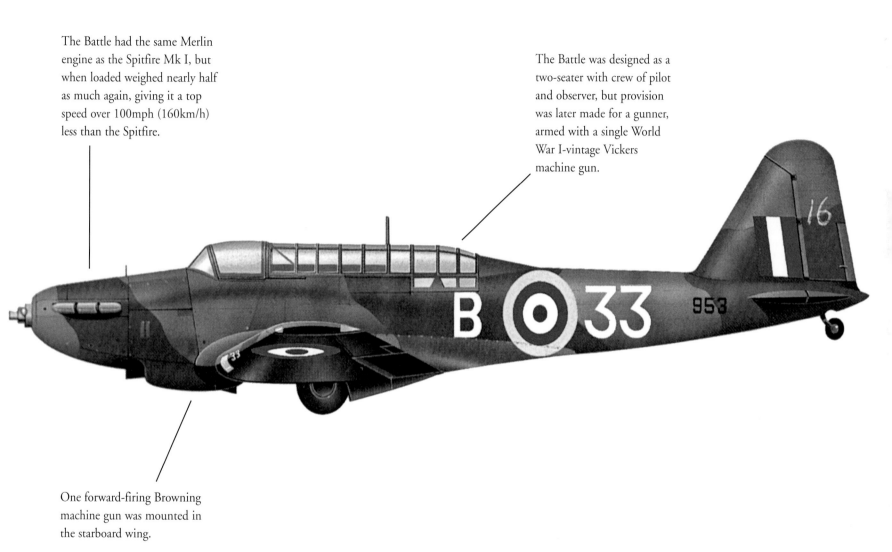

One forward-firing Browning machine gun was mounted in the starboard wing.

FAIREY FULMAR *(1937)*

A naval relative of the Battle, the Fulmar was intended as a long-range carrier fighter to replace such types as the Blackburn Roc, which perhaps was not aiming particularly high. Despite having a slightly more powerful engine than the Battle I and being smaller in all dimensions, the Fulmar's empty weight was over 2,000lb (909kg) greater and so speed and altitude capability was less. Partly this was because of the Admiralty's prewar insistence that all shipboard aircraft carry a navigator to keep the pilot from getting lost. The Fulmar was designed without any rearward-facing armament, operational crews resorted to Tommy guns, flare pistols and in desperation, bundles of toilet paper thrown into the slipstream to confuse a pursuer. Nevertheless, against unescorted bombers, the Fulmar did quite well in protecting Mediterranean convoys, although the best Axis bombers were usually fast enough to escape the plodding fighter.

SPECIFICATIONS (Mk I)

CREW:	2
ENGINE:	one 1080hp (805kW) Rolls-Royce Merlin VIII V-12 piston engine
MAX SPEED:	247mph (398km/h)
SPAN:	46ft 5in (14.15m)
LENGTH:	40ft 2in (12.24m)
HEIGHT:	14ft (4.27m)
WEIGHT:	maximum 10,700lb (4853kg)

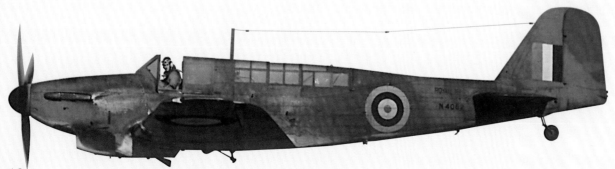

Left: Something of a makeshift solution, the Fulmar could not compete with contemporary land-based fighters, but held the line until 1942 when better types became available.

The Fulmar had essentially the same engine and armament as the early Spitfires, although it was a lot heavier and carried an extra crewman.

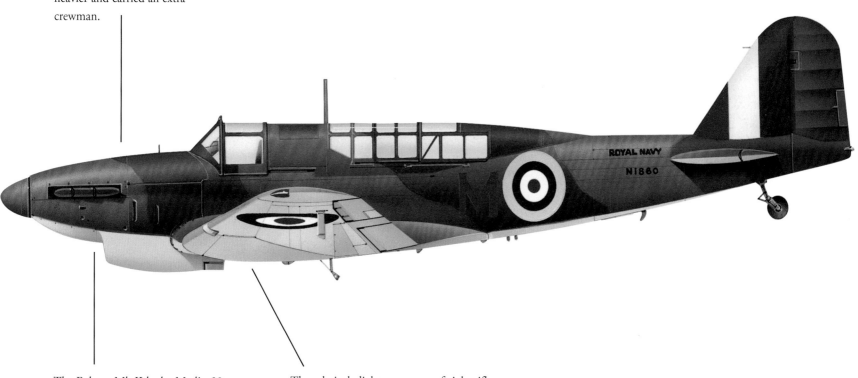

The Fulmar Mk II had a Merlin 30 engine with nearly 300 more horsepower. Despite this, it was only 10mph (16km/h) faster than the Mk I.

The relatively light armament of eight rifle-caliber machine guns and the slow top speed of the Fulmar allowed many German and Italian bombers to get away with limited damage.

ROYAL AIRCRAFT FACTORY B.E.2 *(1912)*

The B.E.2 was designed with emphasis on stability, which made it particularly suitable for reconnaissance for the British Army on the Western Front. In mid-1915 the nature of air war changed with the arrival of the agile Fokker Eindecker with its forward-firing guns. Reconnaissance and bomber aircraft were shot from the skies, with the B.E.2s suffering the worst losses. Reconnaissance aircraft soon needed large escorts, but if a B.E.2 was caught by a fighter, usually all it had to defend itself was pistols or rifles fired by the observer. With the observer in the front, no effective machine-gun arrangement was possible. Continued employment (and production) of B.E.2s in an increasingly dangerous environment led to claims in Parliament that young men were being sent out to be murdered. By 1917 most B.E.2s were found more suitable employment as trainers.

SPECIFICATIONS (B.E.2c)

CREW:	2
ENGINE:	one 90hp (67kW) RAF 1a V-8 piston engine
MAX SPEED:	72mph (116km/h)
SPAN:	36ft 10in (11.23m)
LENGTH:	27ft 3in (8.30m)
HEIGHT:	11ft 4in (3.45m)
WEIGHT:	maximum 2142lb (972kg)

Left: The sedate, stable and very slow B.E.2 made a fine photographic platform in conditions of air superiority, but when Germany fielded the first fighting scouts, the RFC's crews were slaughtered.

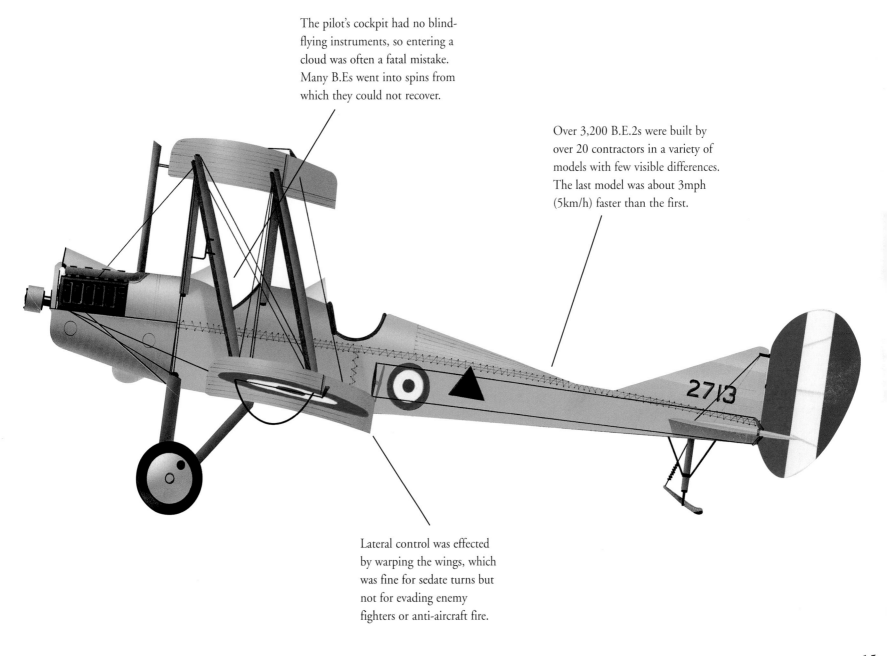

The pilot's cockpit had no blind-flying instruments, so entering a cloud was often a fatal mistake. Many B.Es went into spins from which they could not recover.

Over 3,200 B.E.2s were built by over 20 contractors in a variety of models with few visible differences. The last model was about 3mph (5km/h) faster than the first.

Lateral control was effected by warping the wings, which was fine for sedate turns but not for evading enemy fighters or anti-aircraft fire.

2713

SAUNDERS-ROE PRINCESS *(1952)*

Designed to combine Britain's lead in large flying-boat design with innovations in turbine engine technology, the Princess proved to be a giant white elephant. In 1945 long runways for civil aircraft were still scarce and the Princess seemed like the answer for transatlantic and Empire services. No one really asked what BOAC, the state-owned airline, wanted. Technical problems with the coupled Proteus engines contributed to delays and cost overruns. The first flight date slipped from 1949 to 1952. Costs quadrupled and by 1953 only one small operator was still using flying boats on services out of the UK, BOAC and others having moved on to the new generation of landplanes such as the Boeing Stratocruiser. With no customer, the three prototypes were stored and broken up in 1967.

SPECIFICATIONS

CREW:	6 flight deck and 105 passengers
ENGINE:	ten 3,780hp (2,819kW) Bristol Proteus 2 turboprops arranged as four coupled and two single units
MAX SPEED:	380mph (612km/h)
SPAN:	219ft 6in (66.90m)
LENGTH:	148ft (45.11m)
HEIGHT:	57ft (17.37m)
WEIGHT:	maximum 345,000lb (156,457kg)

Left: The second-biggest flying boat after the "Spruce Goose," the Princess arrived just as large landplanes were coming into their own. Only one prototype of the Princess was completed to fly.

The four inboard nacelle units
were coupled engines driving
contra-rotating propellers.
The outboards were single
engines and propellers.

Despite the obvious
obsolescence of the flying
boat, Saro wanted to build
even bigger jet versions with
up to 1,000 passengers.

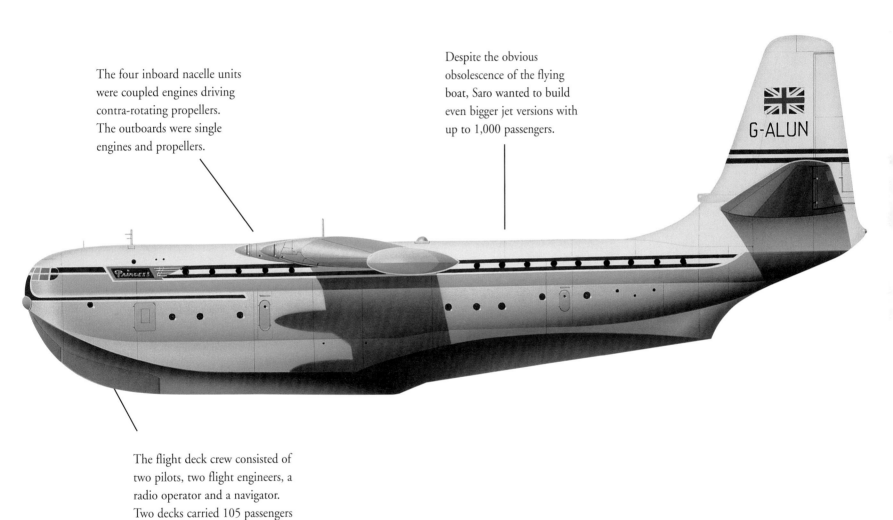

The flight deck crew consisted of
two pilots, two flight engineers, a
radio operator and a navigator.
Two decks carried 105 passengers
in first and tourist class.

SHORT STIRLING (1939)

The Stirling was the first of the RAF's trio of four-engined "heavies." It was always hampered by the RAF's 1936 specifications, which restricted the wingspan to under 100ft (30.48m) to fit into the standard hangars of the day. As such the Stirling was unable to reach the optimum operating altitude of 20,000ft (6,100m) and was a much easier target for flak and fighters than were the Halifax and Lancaster. The prototype was wrecked when its undercarriage collapsed after its first flight. Many teething troubles and accidents delayed the build-up of squadrons, which soon suffered high losses. The new Stirling III introduced in early 1943 remedied some deficiencies, but within five months, 80 percent of these had been lost. Late that year the type was withdrawn from the frontline squadrons.

SPECIFICATIONS (Mk III)

CREW:	7
ENGINE:	four 1,650hp (1,230kW) Bristol Hercules XVI radial engines
MAX SPEED:	270mph (435km/h)
SPAN:	99ft 1in (30.20m)
LENGTH:	87ft 3in (26.59m)
HEIGHT:	22ft 9in (6.93m)
WEIGHT:	maximum 70,000lb (31,751kg)

Left: Compared to the Lancaster and Halifax, the Stirling performed poorly at high altitude and suffered the highest loss rates of the RAF's heavy bombers.

The Stirling used a cut-down version of the wing from the Sunderland flying boat, reduced by over 12ft (4m) in span.

The complicated undercarriage legs were very long to increase the wing incidence and reduce the takeoff run. The length and design of the legs contributed to many accidents.

The size of the bomb bay restricted the weapons that could be carried to nothing larger than 2,000lb (907kg) bombs.

BOGUS CONCEPTS

Here we have aircraft of such variety that it is hard to generalize about the reasons for their failure, but it can be said that they all seemed like good ideas at the time. This category includes a number of radical solutions, some born out of desperation, such as Germany and Japan's manned flying bombs and Japanese fuel-carrying transport that used almost all the fuel en route. Others were solutions looking for a problem such as the Avrocar and the XP-79.

The idea of vertical takeoff (VTO) interceptors able to defend point targets against nuclear-armed bombers obsessed military planners in the early Cold War years. Later the emphasis changed to aircraft that could be dispersed away from vulnerable fixed bases. The quest for VTO aircraft produced a number of "tail-sitters" such as the Pogo, Vertijet and Coléoptère. All of these made transitions from vertical to horizontal flight, where they made pretty mediocre fighters compared with conventional aircraft. Then they had to land while going backward and downward, which proved the Achilles heel of all these designs. Other non-starters include anti-Zeppelin triplanes, jet seaplane fighters, an airplane that mimicked the birds (or at least attempted to), and a genuine flying tank.

Left: One of the most bizarre-looking aircraft ever to have flown, the SNECMA Coléoptère is pictured being prepared for takeoff.

CONVAIR XFY-1 POGO *(1954)*

Along with the Lockheed XFV-1 Salmon, the Convair XFY-1 Pogo was designed as a point defense fighter that could take off and land vertically, using a powerful turboprop with a contra-rotating propeller. Although the idea had some merit, not enough thought was put into how, once the mission was over, the pilot would bring the aircraft back to the landing pad or ship. Wind tunnel tests showed that a rate of descent greater than 10ft (3m) per second could lead to the Pogo tumbling out of control. During the landing, pilot "Skeets" Coleman, the only man to fly the XFY-1, had to look over his shoulder, adjust his ejection seat to 45 degrees and carefully judge the rate of descent while traveling backwards. The unreliability of the T-40 engine and lack of an effective zero-zero ejection seat helped kill the turboprop "tail-sitter" and both the XFY and XFV programs were canceled in mid-1955.

SPECIFICATIONS

CREW:	1
ENGINE:	one 5,850hp (4,362kW) Allison XT-40 turboprop
MAX SPEED:	610mph (982km/h)
SPAN:	27ft 7in (8.43m)
LENGTH:	35ft (10.66m)
TAIL SPAN:	22ft 11in (6.98m)
WEIGHT:	maximum 16,250lb (7,371kg)

Left: The Pogo pilot's life depended entirely on proper functioning of the XT-40 engine, described as "not the world's most reliable." Unlike a helicopter, the XFY-1 could not autorotate to a safe landing.

The propeller was so large because the production version was intended to carry an air-intercept radar, although no mechanism was devised to stop it rotating with the propeller.

To board the Pogo, the pilot had to climb a very tall ladder and lie on his back throughout the start-up and takeoff process. Special moveable hangars were needed so that ground crews could work on the engines.

Although the XFY-1 was never armed, a production Pogo would have had four 0.79in (20mm) cannon or a battery of air-to-air rockets.

Castoring wheels were fitted to the ends of the wings and tail surfaces.

NAVY

XFY-1
138649

23

MCDONNELL XF-85 GOBLIN *(1948)*

The XF-85 Goblin was intended to let heavy bombers bring along their own fighter escort along the lines of various "parasite fighter" experiments conducted with US airships and Soviet bombers in the 1930s. The Goblin itself was designed entirely around the constraints of the bomb bay of the B-36 and thus lacked the performance of a conventional fighter. After fighting off the enemy (with its four machine guns) the Goblin was to return to the bomber and hook on to its trapeze. In its test program, using a B-29, turbulence under the bomber made this very difficult and it was only achieved three times. On another flight the hook broke the canopy and knocked off the pilot's helmet. Experiments were abandoned, but later on modified F-84s were flown under B-36s.

SPECIFICATIONS

CREW:	1
ENGINE:	one 3,000lb (13.4kN) thrust Westinghouse XJ34 turbojet
MAX SPEED:	664mph (1,066km/h)
SPAN:	21ft 1in (6.43m)
LENGTH:	14ft 1in (4.30m)
HEIGHT:	8ft 3in (2.51m)
WEIGHT:	4,550lb (2,063kg)

Left: The XF-85 was only tested from a modified B-29 and never flew under a B-36. Its performance and armament would have been inadequate to deal with the MiG fighters it would have encountered in action.

In front of the cockpit was a large hook on which the XF-85 would be lowered and retrieved in flight.

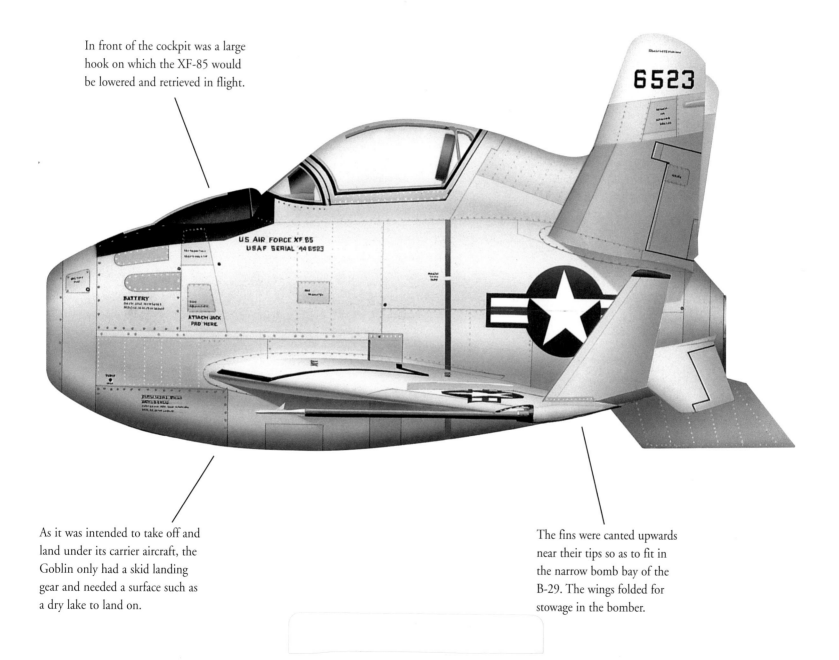

As it was intended to take off and land under its carrier aircraft, the Goblin only had a skid landing gear and needed a surface such as a dry lake to land on.

The fins were canted upwards near their tips so as to fit in the narrow bomb bay of the B-29. The wings folded for stowage in the bomber.

NORTHROP XP-79B *(1945)*

Begun as an extremely ambitious project for a rocket-powered gun-armed interceptor, the XP-79B emerged as a jet, intended to ram enemy bombers and survive due to its strong magnesium structure. This idea, worthy of the Nazis or the Japanese with their backs against the wall, was conceived in the US just as the tide was turning for Allied forces and any need for such desperate measures was waning. The aircraft was not flown until the war was over, and then only once. After a near collision with a fire truck on takeoff, the XP-79 flew well enough for a few minutes until it entered a spin from 8,000ft (2,440m) and crashed at high speed, killing test pilot Harry Crosby. Plans to continue with the rocket-powered versions of the XP-79 ended there, although Northrop's slightly less radical development vehicle, the MX-334 became the first American rocket aircraft.

SPECIFICATIONS

CREW:	1
ENGINE:	two 1150lb (5.1kN) thrust Westinghouse 19B (J30) turbojets
MAX SPEED:	unknown
SPAN:	38ft (11.58m)
LENGTH:	14ft (4.27m)
HEIGHT:	7ft 6in (2.29m)
WEIGHT:	empty 5840lb (2649kg)

Left: One of the first American jet aircraft, the XP-79B had one of the shortest and most spectacular flying careers ever. By the time it was built, the need for a high-speed ramming interceptor was nil.

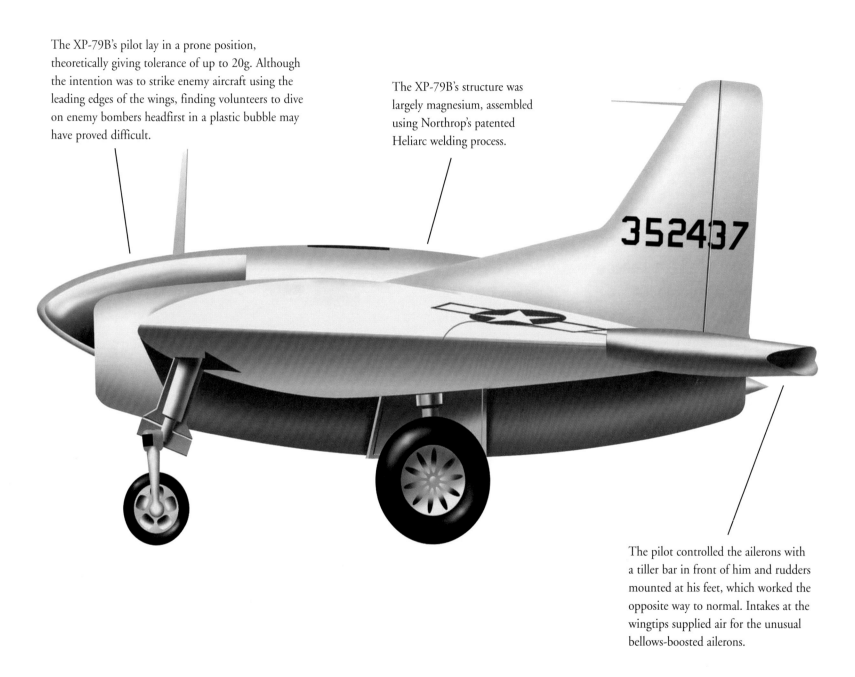

The XP-79B's pilot lay in a prone position, theoretically giving tolerance of up to 20g. Although the intention was to strike enemy aircraft using the leading edges of the wings, finding volunteers to dive on enemy bombers headfirst in a plastic bubble may have proved difficult.

The XP-79B's structure was largely magnesium, assembled using Northrop's patented Heliarc welding process.

The pilot controlled the ailerons with a tiller bar in front of him and rudders mounted at his feet, which worked the opposite way to normal. Intakes at the wingtips supplied air for the unusual bellows-boosted ailerons.

RYAN X-13 VERTIJET *(1955)*

In the early 1950s, some senior officers thought that all US Navy carrier aircraft would be vertical takeoff (VTO) machines within 10 years. They were wrong, but it took such machines as the X-13 Vertijet to prove it. The delta-winged X-13 used a unique landing method, involving a special trailer, a hook and a striped pole. To land the pilot had to approach the trailer's vertical base board without being able to see it. A pole marked with gradations protruded from the board and the pilot had to use this to judge his "altitude" from the landing wire. In one demonstration at the Pentagon, the X-13 flew from its trailer, crossed the Potomac River, destroyed a rose garden with its thrust and landed in a net. Although this impressed the top brass, further funding was not forthcoming and the project petered out.

SPECIFICATIONS

CREW:	1
ENGINE:	one 10,000lb (44.5kN) thrust Rolls-Royce Avon RA.28-49 turbojet
MAX SPEED:	483mph (777km/h)
SPAN:	21ft (6.40m)
LENGTH:	23ft 5in (7.13m)
HEIGHT:	(on wheels) 15ft 2in (4.60m)
WEIGHT:	loaded 7,313lb (3,317kg)

Left: The only successful US jet "tail-sitter," the Vertijet suffered from the same limitations as the Pogo and similar machines. The small payload and short range failed to excite enthusiasm for a production version.

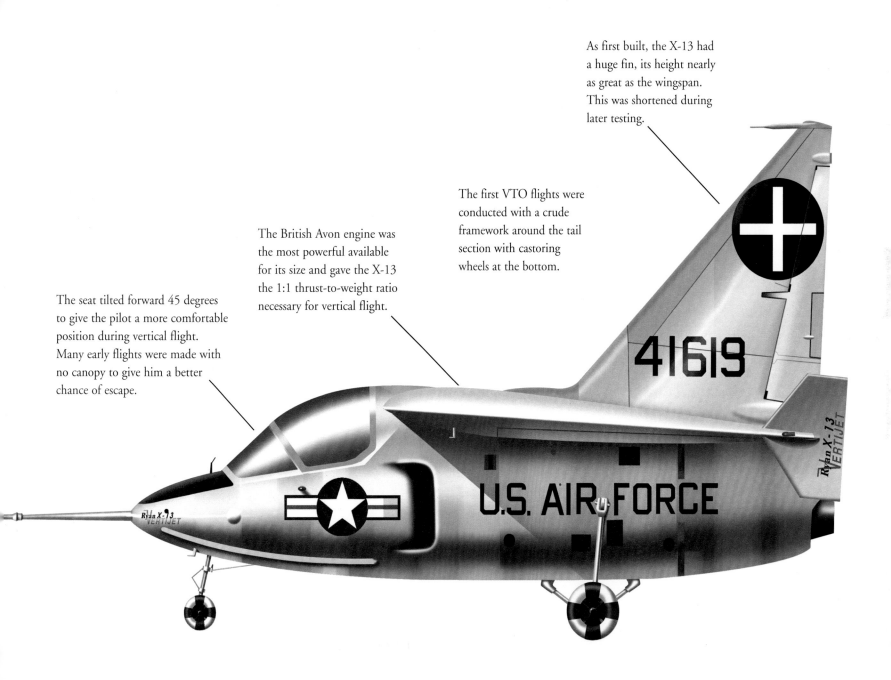

As first built, the X-13 had a huge fin, its height nearly as great as the wingspan. This was shortened during later testing.

The first VTO flights were conducted with a crude framework around the tail section with castoring wheels at the bottom.

The British Avon engine was the most powerful available for its size and gave the X-13 the 1:1 thrust-to-weight ratio necessary for vertical flight.

The seat tilted forward 45 degrees to give the pilot a more comfortable position during vertical flight. Many early flights were made with no canopy to give him a better chance of escape.

41619

U.S. AIR FORCE

Ryan X-13
VERTIJET

SNECMA COLÉOPTÈRE (1959)

ne of the most extraordinary of the 1950s and 60s vertical takeoff (VTO) projects was the French Coléoptère ("annular wing"). The wing design was unique enough, but combining it with a tail-sitting format was a huge technological leap. More or less normal control surfaces directed the aircraft in horizontal flight and thrust vectoring was used to make maneuvers while vertical.

The difficulty with tail-sitting aircraft is landing them, with the pilot looking downward over his shoulder. Transitioning to and from the horizontal to the vertical is also fraught with danger. So it was on only the Coléoptère's ninth flight, when it failed to hover and began to plummet instead, oscillating about all three axes for good measure. The pilot ejected and the Coléoptère shot off at about 50 degrees before crashing, bringing an end to the program.

SPECIFICATIONS

CREW:	1
ENGINE:	one 8,157lb (3,708kg) thrust SNECMA ATAR 101E.V. turbojet
MAX SPEED:	unknown
DIAMETER:	10ft 6in (3.20m)
LENGTH:	26ft 4in (8.02m)
WEIGHT:	maximum 6,614lb (3,000kg)

Left: The Coléoptère proved the feasibility of an annular wing, although it had little opportunity to test it in horizontal flight before crashing during a vertical landing.

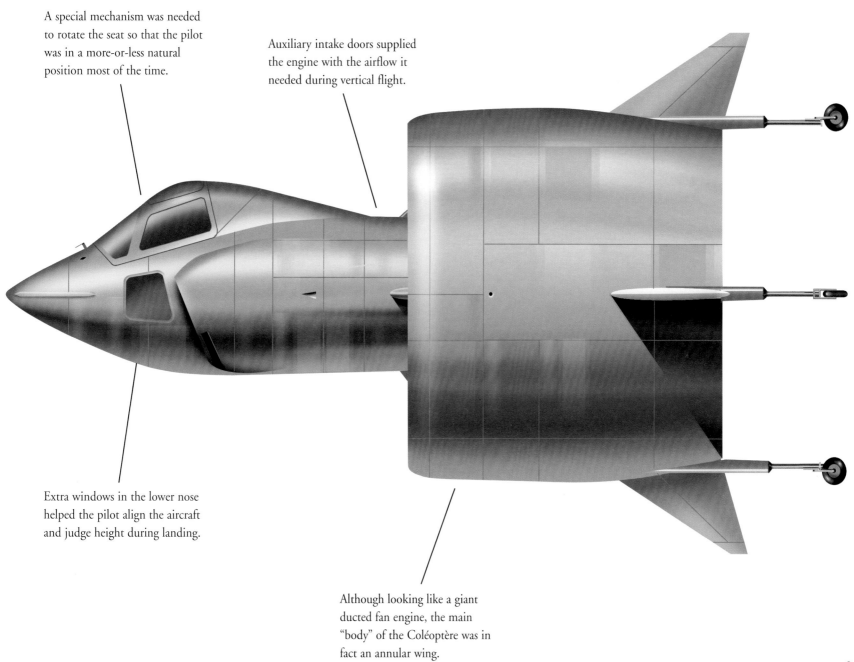

A special mechanism was needed to rotate the seat so that the pilot was in a more-or-less natural position most of the time.

Auxiliary intake doors supplied the engine with the airflow it needed during vertical flight.

Extra windows in the lower nose helped the pilot align the aircraft and judge height during landing.

Although looking like a giant ducted fan engine, the main "body" of the Coléoptère was in fact an annular wing.

TUPOLEV TU-144 *(1968)*

The USSR beat Concorde into the civil supersonic era with the Tupolev 144, which was inevitably dubbed Conkordski. The original Tu-144 design needed extensive modifications, including a new wing before it was ready for airline service. A production Tu-144 broke up and crashed at the 1973 Paris Air Show, killing 14 people.

Due to its turbofan engines the noise produced outside was less than that made by Concorde, but it was louder inside the cabin. The Tu-144 began operations with Aeroflot in 1975, but carrying mail rather than passengers from Moscow to Alma-Ata. The twice-weekly service fell to once a week and was canceled in late 1977. A passenger service on the same route made only 102 flights, with one crash. Mechanical problems made it hard to maintain even one flight per week and services ended in June 1978.

SPECIFICATIONS

CREW:	3 and 140 passengers
ENGINE:	four 44,000lb (20,000kg) thrust Kuzmetsov NK-144 turbofans
CRUISING SPEED:	Mach 2.0 with afterburners
SPAN:	88ft 7in (27.00m)
LENGTH:	215ft 7in (65.70m)
HEIGHT:	42ft 4in (12.90m)
WEIGHT:	396,800lb (180,363kg)

Left: The Tu-144 was bigger and faster than Concorde, but was so mechanically unreliable and inefficient that even the Soviet Union couldn't sustain it in service.

The air conditioning system needed to keep the airframe cool at Mach 2 was ineffective and the cabin was uncomfortably hot. It was also so noisy, along with the engines, that passengers were issued earplugs during flight.

The last of 17 production models were the five Tu-144Ds, which had larger engines and greater range. One was later converted to a flying laboratory and used by NASA for studies of a future SST.

The production aircraft was longer than the prototypes with a more curved wing of greater span and had movable canard surfaces sometimes called "moustaches" behind the cockpit.

POWER PROBLEMS

The engines have been the downfall of many an aircraft. The low output of early engines meant that designers often had to choose between leaving off all excess weight or using as many engines as they could fit aboard, which also multiplied the chance of failures, and every aviator's greatest fear, fires. Many failed projects were sound designs that couldn't wait for the arrival of the right engine. Some were redeemed by application of good engines (and in the case of the Avro Manchester – doubling their number for good measure).

Caproni's experiments into forms of ducted fan piston engines in the 1930s appeared to presage the jet, but produced inferior performance to the equivalent engines in a conventional installation. As such they remained historical curiosities.

Even when the turbine engine began to establish its dominance after World War II, performance was often disappointing. The US Navy was particularly unlucky with the engines it commissioned in the late 1940s and 1950s and wound up with such turkeys as the Westinghouse J34 and J46 turbojets. Of the latter, one Vought Cutlass pilot said that "it put out about as much heat as the same manufacturer's toasters."

Left: Despite its outward similarity to a jet, the Caproni Campini N.1 had poor performance and proved a technological dead end.

BARLING XNBL-1 *(1923)*

Worly War I showed the potential of large aircraft for strategic bombing, but postwar budgets allowed little money for development. The US Army put much of what it had in one giant aeroplane, the Barling XNBL-1 (Experimental Night Bomber Long Range No. 1), usually known as the "Barling Bomber," for there was only ever one.

Although it had six engines and eight propellers, the Barling Bomber's power output was barely adequate to overcome the weight and drag of this massive triplane with its two pilots and five gunners. Theoretically able to carry a 5,000lb (2,268kg) bombload, the XNBL-1 on one occasion failed to get over the Appalachian Mountains between Dayton and Washington D.C. and had to turn back. Funding for an improved version was not forthcoming, but the Barling Bomber carried on to "show the flag" for air power for a number of years.

SPECIFICATIONS

CREW:	7
ENGINE:	six 420hp (313kW) Liberty 12A piston engines
MAX SPEED:	96mph (154km/h)
SPAN:	120ft (36.58m)
LENGTH:	65ft (19.81m)
HEIGHT:	27ft (8.23m)
WEIGHT:	loaded 42,569lb (19,309kg)

Left: Designed by Walter Barling, who was responsible for the Tarrant Tabor, and promoted by the controversial General Billy Mitchell, the XNBL-1 redefined the word cumbersome. At least by this time some lessons of balance had been learned and the Barling had a relatively long and safe, if totally undistinguished, career.

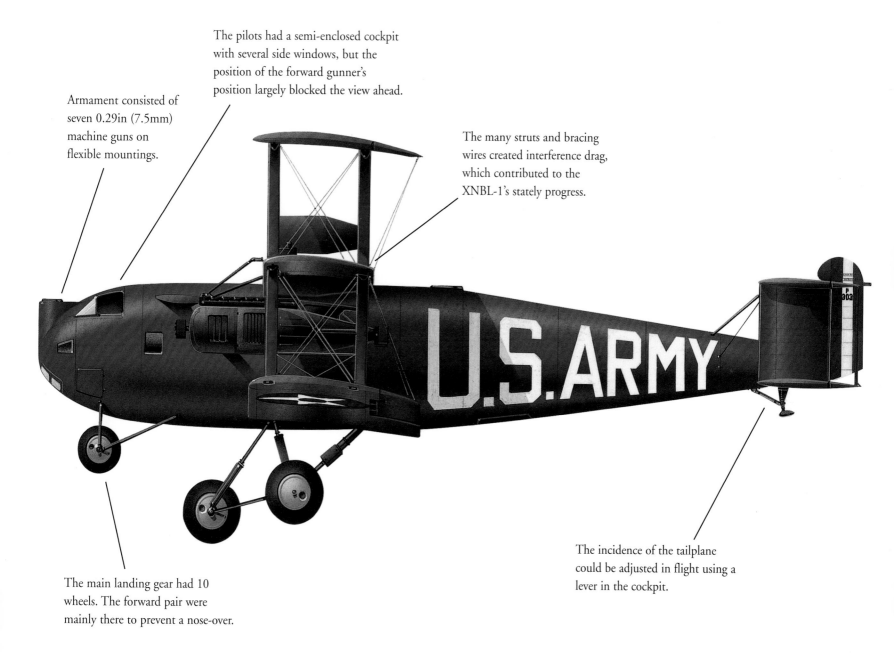

The pilots had a semi-enclosed cockpit with several side windows, but the position of the forward gunner's position largely blocked the view ahead.

Armament consisted of seven 0.29in (7.5mm) machine guns on flexible mountings.

The many struts and bracing wires created interference drag, which contributed to the XNBL-1's stately progress.

U.S. ARMY

The main landing gear had 10 wheels. The forward pair were mainly there to prevent a nose-over.

The incidence of the tailplane could be adjusted in flight using a lever in the cockpit.

BRISTOL 188 *(1962)*

The Bristol 188, sometimes called the "flaming pencil," was designed to research structures for sustained supersonic flight, particularly in support of the Avro 730 reconnaissance aircraft. This required the aircraft to "soak" at Mach 2.6 for at least 30 minutes. To achieve the required strength the structure was largely stainless steel, which required new techniques and great expense to fabricate into an airframe.

Takeoff speed was nearly 300mph (483km/h), but in all other respects the 188's speed was slower than desired, being able to achieve Mach 2.0 for only a couple of minutes. The whole project cost a huge amount and failed to achieve its objectives. It was wound down rather than develop the engines further. Test pilot Godfrey Auty was voted the "man most likely to eject in the coming year" by his peers but thankfully never had to.

SPECIFICATIONS

CREW:	1
ENGINE:	two 14,000lb (62.28kN) thrust de Havilland Gyron Junior PS.50 afterburning turbojets
MAX SPEED:	Mach 1.88
SPAN:	35ft 1in (10.69m)
LENGTH:	77ft 8in (23.67m)
HEIGHT:	12ft (3.65m)
WEIGHT:	unknown

Left: The stainless steel 188 certainly looked futuristic. By the time it was completed, the aircraft it was supposed to provide data for had been canceled. The project lasted from 1953 to 1964 with the two aircraft flying for less than two years.

A new type of stainless steel, joined by a new "puddle" welding process was needed for the 188. It took over two years to develop the steel before it could even be ordered for construction use.

The PS.50 (modified Gyron Junior) engines had greater diameter than the fuselage but never developed enough thrust to push the 188 to the high speeds required.

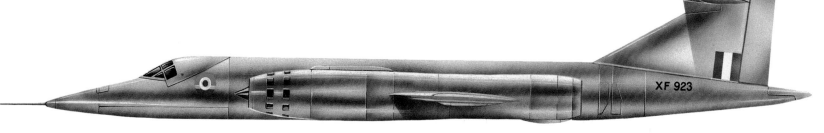

XF 923

Fuel capacity was usually only enough for 20–25 minutes of flight including a high-speed run. By airline standards the 188 was in a fuel emergency situation before takeoff.

CAPRONI CAMPINI N.1 *(1940)*

In 1939 inventor Secondo Campini convinced the Caproni company to build an airframe to test his new power unit that he believed would replace the propeller. The Italian aircraft industry had decided that a gas turbine engine was impractical (even as German and British scientists were testing theirs). The Caproni Campini N.1 flew in 1940 and has sometimes been touted as the world's first jet aircraft. It was nothing of the sort – power came from a relatively small piston engine inside the forward fuselage, which turned a variable-pitch compressor in what we would today call a ducted fan. A rudimentary form of afterburner allowed fuel to be burned in a propelling nozzle to give some extra thrust. Despite this, the N.1 would only make 233mph (375km/h), slower than the Fiat CR.42 biplane.

SPECIFICATIONS

CREW:	2
ENGINE:	one 900hp (671kW) Isotta-Fraschini radial engine driving a three-stage fan compressor
MAX SPEED:	233mph (375km/h)
SPAN:	52ft (15.85m)
LENGTH:	43ft (13.10m)
HEIGHT:	15ft 5in (4.70m)
WEIGHT:	9,250lb (4,195kg)

Left: The FAI acknowledged the N.1 as the first jet-propelled aircraft, but were unaware of the secretly flown Heinkel 178. A more powerful supercharged engine might have made a difference to the N.1's pedestrian performance, but wartime pressures brought an end to development.

The low power of the N.1's piston engine kept it below 13,124ft (4,000m), where the ducted fan arrangement would have been effective.

The N.1's power system had no hot compressor section. The cold compressed air was ducted and mixed with jet fuel and ignited, giving extra thrust.

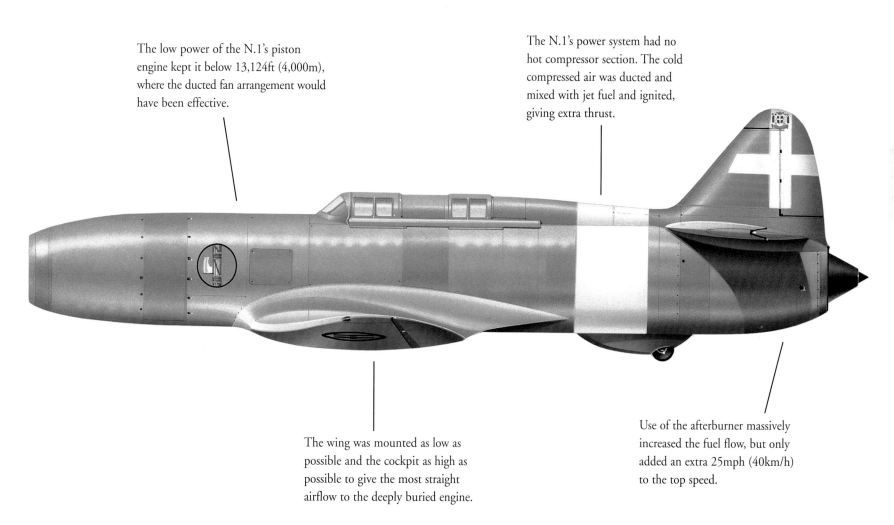

The wing was mounted as low as possible and the cockpit as high as possible to give the most straight airflow to the deeply buried engine.

Use of the afterburner massively increased the fuel flow, but only added an extra 25mph (40km/h) to the top speed.

DOUGLAS X-3 STILETTO *(1952)*

The US Air Force, Navy and NACA (predecessor to NASA) all invested in this extraordinary research craft that looked like it was going supersonic while sitting on the ground, but barely achieved it in the air. Many new construction techniques and materials were needed to build the X-3 to withstand its anticipated flight regime, and large amounts of expensive titanium were used. Unfortunately, engine choice was the Westinghouse J34, one of several turbojets built by this company that failed to perform as advertised.

Although the airframe was designed to reach Mach 2.2, the best it ever achieved was Mach 1.21, in a dive. This meant it achieved little toward its objective of studying kinetic heating research. The USAF only flew the X-3 six times before handing it to NACA, who made but 20 more flights before it wound up in a museum.

SPECIFICATIONS

CREW:	1
ENGINE:	two 4,200lb (18.68kN) thrust Westinghouse J34 turbojets
MAX SPEED:	706mph (1,136km/h)
SPAN:	21ft 8in (6.91m)
LENGTH:	66ft 9in (20.35m)
HEIGHT:	12ft 6in (3.81m)
WEIGHT:	loaded 22,400lb (10,160kg)

Left: Intended to explore high-speed high-altitude flight, the X-3 was one of many 1950s aircraft crippled by useless Westinghouse engines and only one of the intended three prototypes was built.

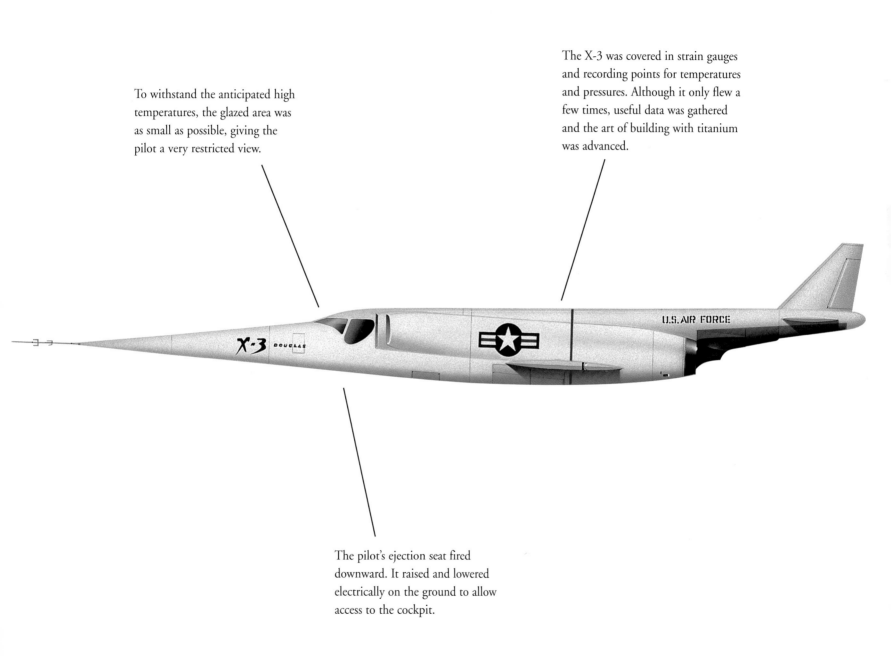

To withstand the anticipated high temperatures, the glazed area was as small as possible, giving the pilot a very restricted view.

The X-3 was covered in strain gauges and recording points for temperatures and pressures. Although it only flew a few times, useful data was gathered and the art of building with titanium was advanced.

The pilot's ejection seat fired downward. It raised and lowered electrically on the ground to allow access to the cockpit.

X-3 DOUGLAS

U.S. AIR FORCE

HUGHES XF-11 *(1946)*

Designed to meet the same specification as the Republic XF-12, the XF-11 was said to be scaled up from the mysterious D-2 fighter that Howard Hughes flew in secret in 1943. Resembling an enlarged P-38 Lightning, the XF-11 was optimized for the high-altitude photo-reconnaissance role. Under pressure from Congress to deliver on this project and the equally late "Spruce Goose," Howard Hughes himself made the XF-11's first flight. Unwisely for a maiden flight, Hughes stayed up much longer than planned – until one propeller went into reverse pitch and the XF-11 crashed into an unoccupied house in Beverly Hills. Hughes survived with head injuries, but some say he never really recovered. The second aircraft was evaluated by the USAF, who, after deciding it was twice as expensive, harder to operate and inferior to the XR-12 Rainbow, terminated the program.

SPECIFICATIONS

CREW:	2
ENGINE:	two 3,000hp (2,238kW) Pratt & Whitney R-4360-37 radial piston engines
MAX SPEED:	unknown
SPAN:	101ft (30.78m)
LENGTH:	65ft 5in (20.15m)
HEIGHT:	unknown
WEIGHT:	maximum 58,300lb (26,444kg)

Left: Howard Hughes' XF-11 nearly cost him his life. Some say it cost him his sanity. It certainly had its faults, but the USAF could have used a purpose-built aircraft in its class in the 1950s.

The XF-11 had a two-man
cockpit and a large camera nose.
Unlike the XF-12 there was no
room for onboard film processing.

The ailerons were small and
gave sluggish control at low
altitudes, although high-altitude
performance was very good.

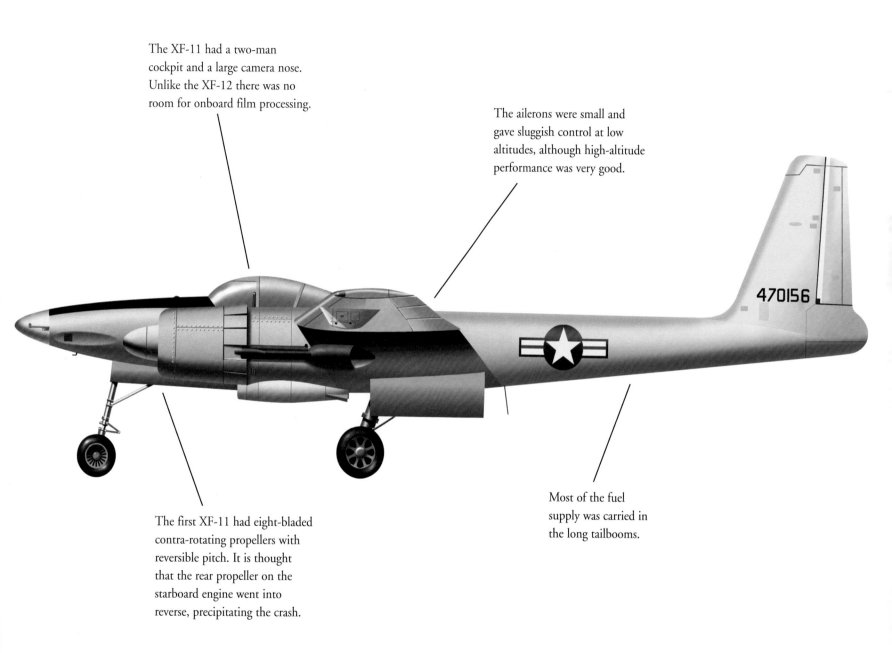

470156

The first XF-11 had eight-bladed
contra-rotating propellers with
reversible pitch. It is thought
that the rear propeller on the
starboard engine went into
reverse, precipitating the crash.

Most of the fuel
supply was carried in
the long tailbooms.

MESSERSCHMITT ME 163 KOMET *(1941)*

The Komet was the world's first (and so far only) operational rocket-powered fighter. Although the prototype Me 163A first flew in August 1941, it was not until February 1944 that production Me 163Bs entered service in any number, official disinterest playing a part in the slow progress of development. Although its performance was fantastic, the Komet carried only enough fuel for four minutes' powered flying. The fuel was an extremely volatile cocktail mixed in flight, which would in the wrong proportions readily explode. Unlike some other Luftwaffe "last ditch" aircraft, the Komet required exceptional piloting skills, particularly on landing, and a shortage of trained pilots restricted deployment as much as did fuel supplies or production delays. Destruction of the fuel plant by bombing added to the Me 163 squadrons' woes in the last months of the war. Each mission, however, saw the available aircraft and pilot numbers reduced by fighters, off-field landings and landing crashes.

SPECIFICATIONS
(Me 163B-1a)

CREW:	1
ENGINE:	one 3,748lb (16.67kN) thrust Walter rocket motor
MAX SPEED:	597mph (960km/h)
SPAN:	30ft 7in (9.40m)
LENGTH:	19ft 2in (5.85m)
HEIGHT:	9ft (2.76m)
WEIGHT:	loaded 9,502lb (4310kg)

Left: With a range of only 25 miles (40km), the Komet was only good for point defense. Once combat was over, the pilot faced the most dangerous part of the mission – a safe landing.

Armament was two powerful but slow-firing 1.18in (30mm) cannon. The pilot had little time to aim and hold his fire before he was past the target. One or two hits was usually enough to destroy a bomber, however.

The fuels in the Komet were highly corrosive and would dissolve organic material (such as the pilot). To avoid this, the pilots would wear special asbestos fiber suits.

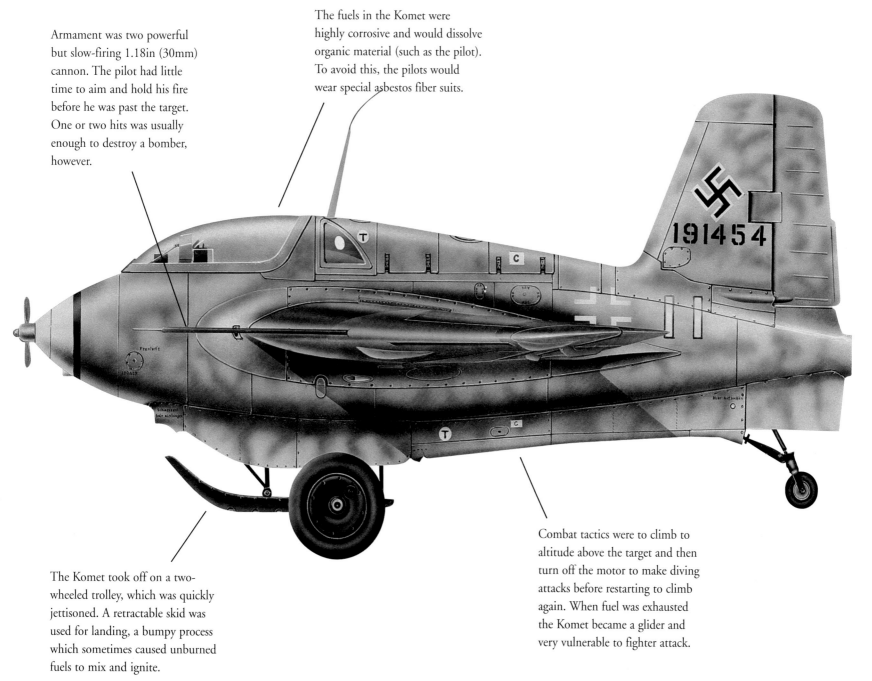

The Komet took off on a two-wheeled trolley, which was quickly jettisoned. A retractable skid was used for landing, a bumpy process which sometimes caused unburned fuels to mix and ignite.

Combat tactics were to climb to altitude above the target and then turn off the motor to make diving attacks before restarting to climb again. When fuel was exhausted the Komet became a glider and very vulnerable to fighter attack.

47

VOUGHT F7U CUTLASS *(1948)*

Seeing that the lead in fighter development was falling to the Air Force, the traditionally conservative US Navy ordered the radical swept-wing, twin-tailed Cutlass in 1946. It was an extremely aerodynamically advanced and mechanically complicated aircraft for its day. All three of the initial XF7U-1 prototypes crashed. The Cutlass failed its carrier suitability tests and the initial model was retrospectively designated an "experimental" type. A complete redesign produced the production F7U-3, which proved short-ranged and maintenance intensive. The Cutlass had a complicated hydraulic system, temperamental engines, weak landing gear, and to top it off, unreliable ejection seats. The Cutlass is usually remembered for its poor safety record, with over a quarter of the 300 F7Us built being lost or involved in serious accidents.

SPECIFICATIONS (F7U-3)

CREW:	1
ENGINE:	two 4,600lb (20.5kN) thrust Westinghouse J46-WE-8A afterburning turbojets
MAX SPEED:	680mph (1,095km/h)
SPAN:	38ft 8in (11.70m)
LENGTH:	44ft 3in (13.40m)
HEIGHT:	14ft 7in (4.40m)
WEIGHT:	loaded 31,642lb (14,350kg)

Left: The Cutlass has been called "the least safe US Navy fighter ever flown."

When the hydraulics failed a manual control system kicked in, but only after 11 seconds, during which the Cutlass went where it had last been pointed.

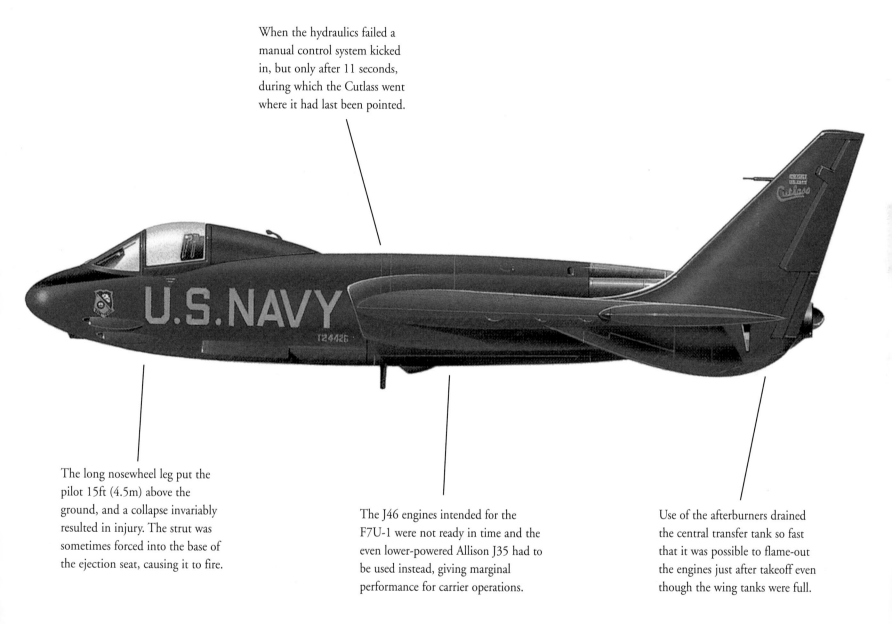

U.S. NAVY

The long nosewheel leg put the pilot 15ft (4.5m) above the ground, and a collapse invariably resulted in injury. The strut was sometimes forced into the base of the ejection seat, causing it to fire.

The J46 engines intended for the F7U-1 were not ready in time and the even lower-powered Allison J35 had to be used instead, giving marginal performance for carrier operations.

Use of the afterburners drained the central transfer tank so fast that it was possible to flame-out the engines just after takeoff even though the wing tanks were full.

49

BEECHCRAFT STARSHIP 2000A *(1986)*

To prove the concept of an all-composite replacement for the King Air, Beechcraft commissioned Burt Rutan's Scaled Composites company to build an 85 percent size proof-of-concept aircraft. When it first appeared at a business aircraft exhibition it caused a sensation, but this was little more than a "flying wind-tunnel model" and was very far from a certificated aircraft. Beech announced an ambitious schedule for certification, but subcontractors let them down and they had to develop the techniques for fabricating and molding high-tech materials themselves. As with the LearFan, the FAA insisted on a very rigorous testing program, including subjecting a test airframe to two simulated lifetimes (40,000 hours) of stress and insisting on extra lightning protection. After a five-and-a-half year development program that cost over $300 million, only 53 production aircraft were built, and many were never sold, in part due to economic recession.

SPECIFICATIONS

CREW:	2
ENGINE:	two 1,200hp (895kW) Pratt & Whitney Canada PT6A-67A turboprops
MAX SPEED:	385mph (620km/h)
SPAN:	54ft 5in (16.60m)
LENGTH:	46ft 1in (14.05m)
HEIGHT:	12ft 11in (3.94m)
WEIGHT:	loaded 14,900lb (6758kg)

Left: The first all-composite business aircraft actually certified in the USA, the Starship was one of the most thoroughly tested aircraft ever. To avoid product liability issues and to stop manufacturing unprofitable spare parts, Beech has tried to buy back all the Starships in use and scrap them, but many of the owners have resisted the offer.

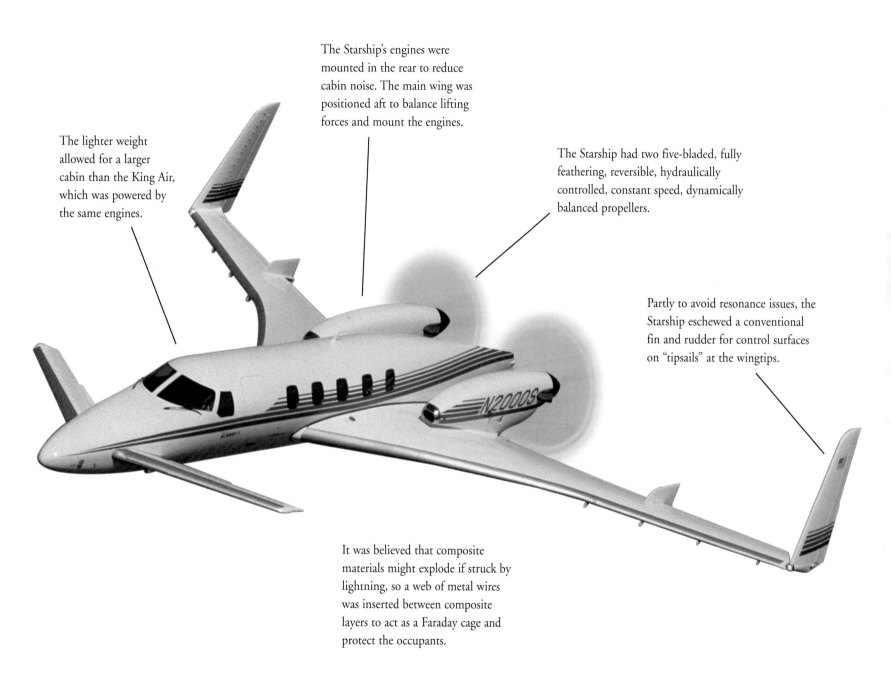

The lighter weight allowed for a larger cabin than the King Air, which was powered by the same engines.

The Starship's engines were mounted in the rear to reduce cabin noise. The main wing was positioned aft to balance lifting forces and mount the engines.

The Starship had two five-bladed, fully feathering, reversible, hydraulically controlled, constant speed, dynamically balanced propellers.

Partly to avoid resonance issues, the Starship eschewed a conventional fin and rudder for control surfaces on "tipsails" at the wingtips.

It was believed that composite materials might explode if struck by lightning, so a web of metal wires was inserted between composite layers to act as a Faraday cage and protect the occupants.

BOEING/SIKORSKY RAH-66 COMANCHE *(1996)*

The Comanche was intended to replace the US Army's relatively unsophisticated OH-58D Kiowa Warrior and AH-1 Cobra with a stealthy multi-sensor platform able to carry out scouting and attack missions, shoot down enemy helicopters and pass data directly to the Longbow Apache attack helicopter. Slow funding of the program encouraged more roles and capabilities to be added, increasing the weight and cost. An early plan envisaged procurement of as many as 5,023 Comanches, later reduced to 1,400, then 1,213 and finally 650. As the numbers fell, the per-unit cost rose from $12.1 million to $58.9 million. In the end, 16 years and the expenditure of $8 billion only achieved little more than two flying prototypes and a partially completed test program.

SPECIFICATIONS

CREW:	2
ENGINE:	two 1,432hp (1,069kW) T800-LHTEC-801 turboshafts
MAX SPEED:	204mph (328km/h)
ROTOR DIAMETER:	39ft 1in (11.90m)
LENGTH:	46ft 10in (14.28m)
HEIGHT:	11ft 2in (3.39m)
WEIGHT:	maximum 17,174lb (7790kg)

Left: Initiated in 1988, the RAH-66's first flight did not take place until 1996 and the whole thing was canceled in February 2004. The US Army will put the money into buying 800 new helicopters and modernizing another 1,400.

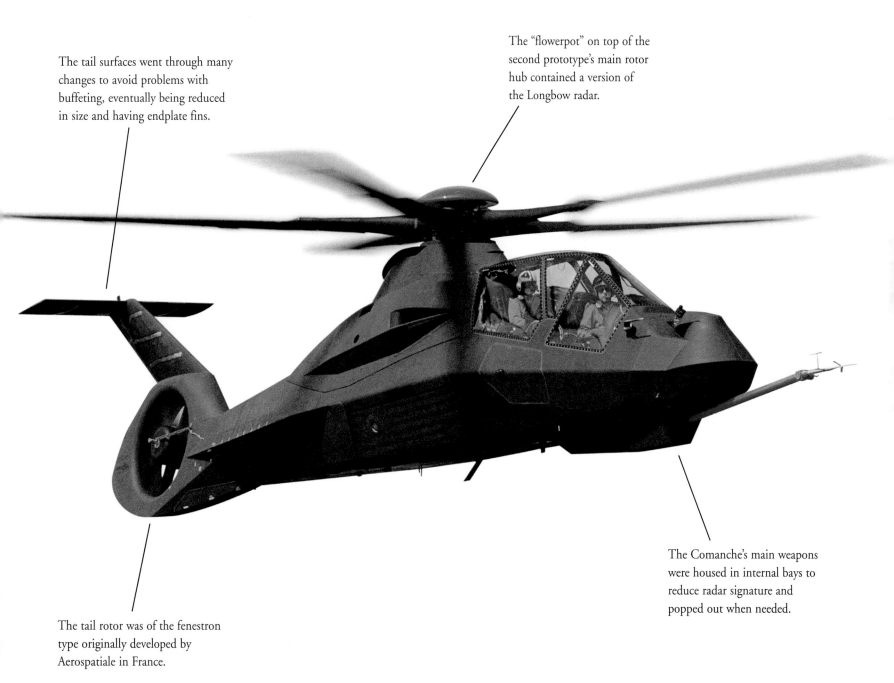

The tail surfaces went through many changes to avoid problems with buffeting, eventually being reduced in size and having endplate fins.

The "flowerpot" on top of the second prototype's main rotor hub contained a version of the Longbow radar.

The tail rotor was of the fenestron type originally developed by Aerospatiale in France.

The Comanche's main weapons were housed in internal bays to reduce radar signature and popped out when needed.

DE HAVILLAND COMET I *(1949)*

The first flight of the Comet jetliner in 1949 put Britain five years ahead of the USA in civil aviation development. Two Comet 1 crashes caused mainly by pilot error were followed by two mysterious disappearances over the Mediterranean. Public confidence plummeted and a Comet airframe was tested to destruction to establish the cause, proving that inflight breakup had been caused by metal fatigue springing from window corners and other angular apertures.

Before these tests were done a further Comet disintegrated, dooming future sales of the Comet 1. Only a few Comet 2s were built for the RAF. The Comet 4 (with round windows) was a bigger, better product, but by the time it appeared the USA, France and the USSR had stolen a march on the UK, from which it never quite recovered.

SPECIFICATIONS

CREW:	7 and 36 passengers
ENGINE:	four 5,013lb (22.3kN) thrust de Havilland Ghost 50-Mk1 turbojets
CRUISING SPEED:	450mph (724km/h)
SPAN:	114ft 10in (35m)
LENGTH:	111ft 6in (34m)
HEIGHT:	29ft 6in (9.1m)
WEIGHT:	162,000lb (73,482kg)

Left: Knowledge of metal fatigue and the effects of repeated pressurization on airframes was limited when the Comet was built. The findings of the investigation improved the design of future aircraft.

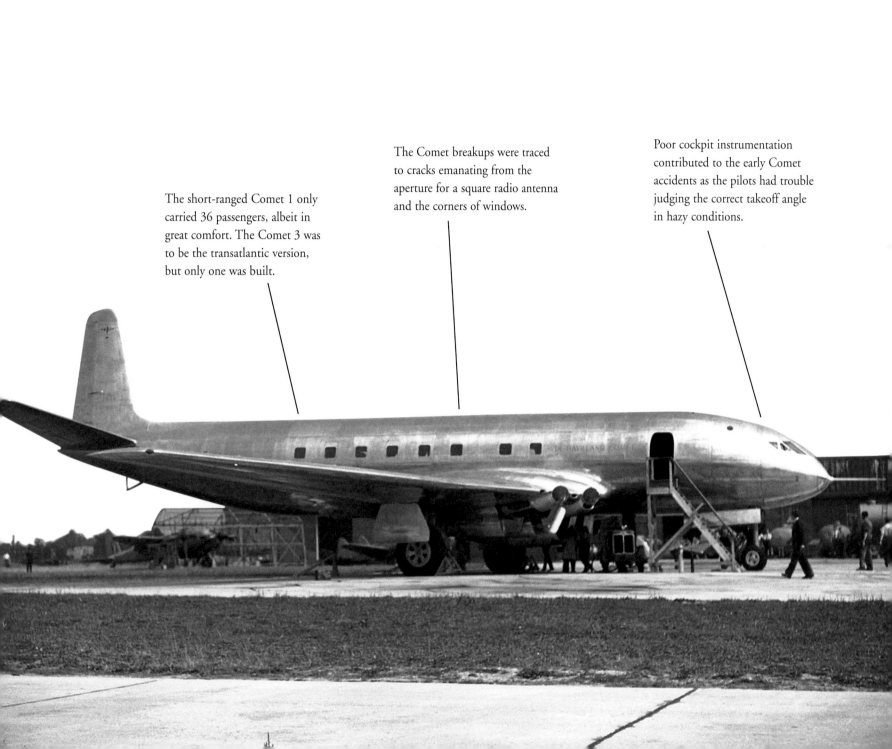

The short-ranged Comet 1 only carried 36 passengers, albeit in great comfort. The Comet 3 was to be the transatlantic version, but only one was built.

The Comet breakups were traced to cracks emanating from the aperture for a square radio antenna and the corners of windows.

Poor cockpit instrumentation contributed to the early Comet accidents as the pilots had trouble judging the correct takeoff angle in hazy conditions.

DE HAVILLAND D.H.91 ALBATROSS *(1937)*

Originally built as a fast mailplane for the transatlantic run, the beautiful Albatross was beset with structural and mechanical problems and just plain bad luck. The wooden monocoque fuselage tapered smoothly to the tail, but it wasn't very strong. On the second aircraft's third landing the rear fuselage broke in two. The Albatross's landing gear gave endless problems – not lowering, collapsing and suffering brake failures. Two mailplanes and five airliners for Imperial Airways were built. The former were impressed into RAF service in 1940 for use on the Iceland run. Both were written off after landing accidents. Fires, accidents and enemy action befell the Imperial aircraft. The final two D.H.91s were scrapped in 1943, it having been discovered that the spars had rotted.

SPECIFICATIONS

CREW:	4
ENGINE:	four 525hp (391kW) de Havilland Gypsy 12 piston engines
MAX SPEED:	225mph (362km/h)
SPAN:	105ft (32m)
LENGTH:	71ft 6in (21.79m)
HEIGHT:	22ft 8in (6.78m)
WEIGHT:	maximum 29,500lb (13,381kg)

Left: The shapely lines of the Albatross concealed serious structural weaknesses. Only seven were built, one of the lowest totals of any de Havilland production aircraft.

The fuselage was made of laminations of cedar ply and balsa wood, built as a monocoque in which the skins bore the load.

As first built the Albatross had tailfins inset near the fuselage, but directional instability saw a change to more traditional endplate fins.

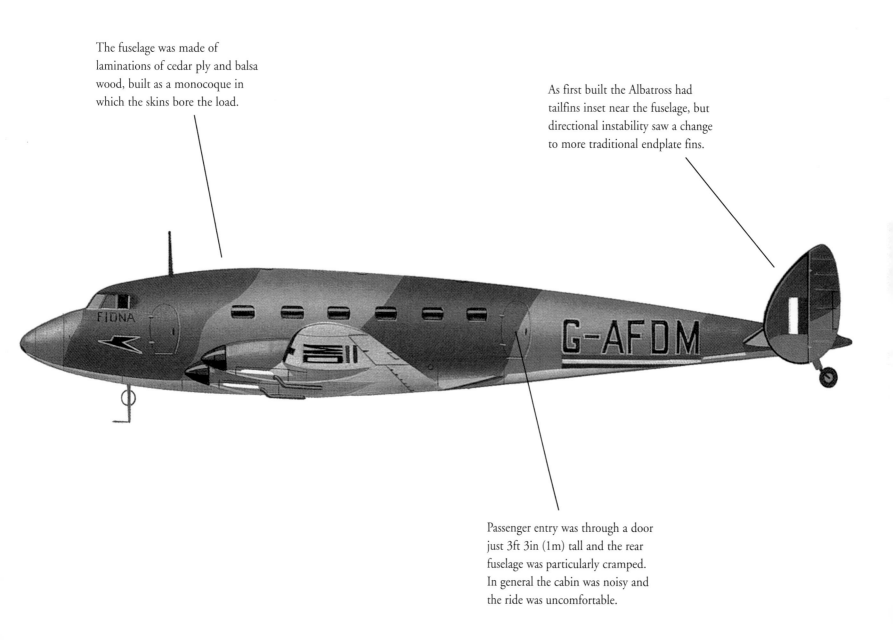

Passenger entry was through a door just 3ft 3in (1m) tall and the rear fuselage was particularly cramped. In general the cabin was noisy and the ride was uncomfortable.

FOCKE-WULF FW 200 CONDOR (1937)

Gaining the reputation as the "scourge of the Atlantic" when it appeared, the Condor maritime patrol bomber was an overloaded lash-up of a long-range airliner design. Designed to operate at weights and stresses expected in civil transport use, the design was not up to pulling *g* and carrying bombs, guns and armor. More than half of the aircraft delivered in 1940 suffered structural failure. In particular, the rear fuselage was weak and prone to fracture.

By the time the improved models entered service in 1941, they faced greatly improved convoy defenses, including ship-based fighters and well-armed patrol aircraft like Sunderlands and Liberators. Serviceability fell and many aircraft were called away to the Eastern Front where they were used as transports for the supply of encircled Stalingrad, a role to which they were poorly suited.

SPECIFICATIONS (200C-3/U4)

CREW:	7
ENGINE:	four 1,200hp (895kW) BMW-Bramo 323R-2 Fafnir piston engines
MAX SPEED:	224mph (360km/h)
SPAN:	107ft 9in (32.85m)
LENGTH:	76ft 11in (23.45m)
HEIGHT:	20ft 8in (6.30m)
WEIGHT:	maximum 50,057lb (24,520kg)

Left: A sight common on the Luftwaffe airfields along the Bay of Biscay was that of a Condor that had literally "cracked up" on landing when its weak rear fuselage was overstressed.

The sleek airliner design was soon encumbered by gun turrets, a ventral gondola and in some cases radar aerials.

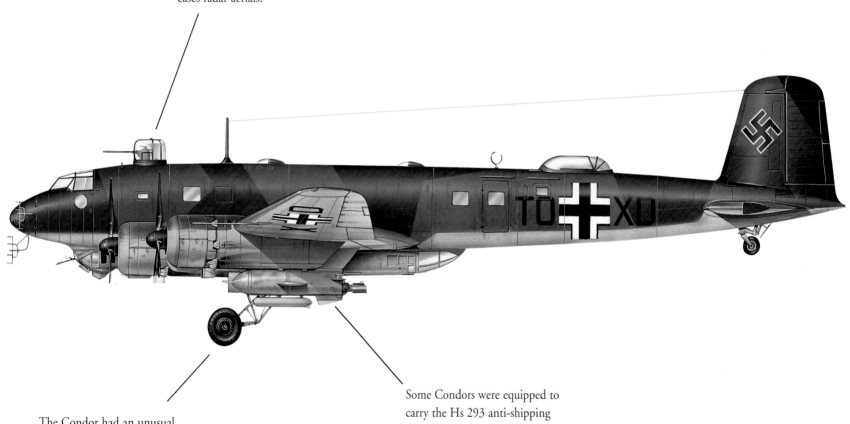

The Condor had an unusual forward-retracting main undercarriage with double wheels. This would lock into place with air pressure when loaded.

Some Condors were equipped to carry the Hs 293 anti-shipping missile under the outer engines. Otherwise they carried up to 4,630lb (2,100kg) of bombs.

ROYAL AIRCRAFT FACTORY RE.8 *(1916)*

Astately and stable observation and photo-reconnaissance platform, the RAF RE.8 was designed to replace the slow and vulnerable BE.2 with an aircraft of superior performance and armament. The actual improvements were marginal, but at least the observer was now located in the seat with a view. The RE.8 rarely achieved anything like its stated top speed. The difference between the actual combat speed and the stalling speed was only about 20mph (32km/h). Maneuvers had to be made carefully so as not to fall into a deadly spin. The high stalling speed also made landings difficult and dangerous. The armament was useless for either offense or defense. RE.8s fell in great numbers to German fighters. Manfred von Richthofen, the "Red Baron," shot down seven of them, but didn't regard them as much sport.

SPECIFICATIONS

CREW:	2
ENGINE:	one 150hp (112kW) Royal Aircraft Factory 4a inline piston engine
MAX SPEED:	103mph (166km/h)
SPAN:	42ft 7in (12.98m)
LENGTH:	27ft 11in (8.50m)
HEIGHT:	11ft 5in (3.47m)
WEIGHT:	loaded 2,678lb (1,215kg)

Left: Nicknamed the "Harry Tate" after a popular music hall comedian, aircrews found flying the RE.8 anything but amusing. Despite their pedestrian performance and vulnerability, over 4,000 were built.

The RE.8 had a forward-firing machine gun set at an angle so the pilot could fire it, but where the bullets would miss the propeller. This made hitting an opponent almost impossible.

At least on early model RE.8s the observer could not turn around in his seat or fire the rear gun from a standing position, so he had to somehow aim and fire it over his shoulder.

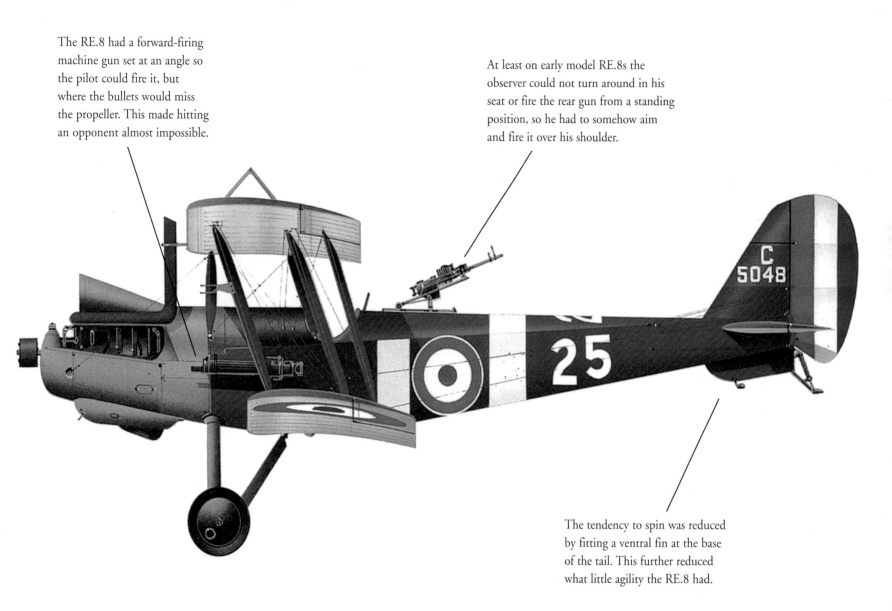

The tendency to spin was reduced by fitting a ventral fin at the base of the tail. This further reduced what little agility the RE.8 had.

UNINTENTIONALLY UNSTABLE

Today computers keep the current generation of combat aircraft on the straight and level or under control at the very limits of their physical flight envelopes. Without computerized systems they will not remain in control (or one piece) for a moment. This is often called relaxed stability. Earlier generations of aircraft had examples of this too, but normally unintentionally.

This section contains three World War I biplanes that had trouble taking off. Two of these (the De Bruyère C 1 and Tarrant Tabor) were so unstable in pitch or top-heavy that they tipped over on their maiden flight attempts. The Lohner Type AA was so close-coupled that it was impossible to keep straight at takeoff speeds – this was a problem even when aerodromes were just big fields.

Instability in yaw (poor directional control) seems to have been the most common problem, particularly with production aircraft, but unwanted pitch movement was more likely to be dangerous, or downright deadly. The Flying Flea and Flying Bedstead shared something more than just similar names – it was terribly easy to tip both of them into a position from which they could not recover, with a crash the inevitable result.

Left: Without the benefit of the computerized control system used in the modern B-2 Spirit, the XB-35 was dangerously unstable.

CURTISS SB2C HELLDIVER (1940)

A successor to the aging but worthy SBD Dauntless dive-bomber, the Helldiver was built in large numbers but never totally supplanted the "Slow But Deadly." Huge orders were made even before the first flight of the XSB2C-1 prototype, which exhibited poor handling and stability and very poor stall characteristics. The prototype crashed but was rebuilt, achieving the feat of having many changes but little visible difference before it crashed again. Sensibly the Royal Navy rejected the Helldiver, but the US committed to mass production from three factories. Production models proved in some ways worse than the prototype and inferior in many to the Dauntless. By 1944 it was in action in the Pacific, suffering many inflight breakups and deck landing accidents, although slowly proving its worth as a bomber. It had to, as the staggering total of over 7,100 were built, making it the most numerous dive-bomber ever.

SPECIFICATIONS

CREW:	2
ENGINE:	one 1,900hp (1,417kW) Wright R-2800-20 Cyclone radial engine
MAX SPEED:	293mph (472km/h)
SPAN:	49ft 9in (15.14m)
LENGTH:	36ft 8in (11.18m)
HEIGHT:	14ft 9in (4.49m)
WEIGHT:	maximum 16,750lb (7,598kg)

Left: Affected by a very rigid specification, a weak structure and poor stability, the Helldiver was extremely unpopular with all but the most experienced pilots.

The fuselage was lengthened and the tail enlarged following stability problems with the prototype.

Reliability was poor and handling was tricky, leading to the nickname "Beast."

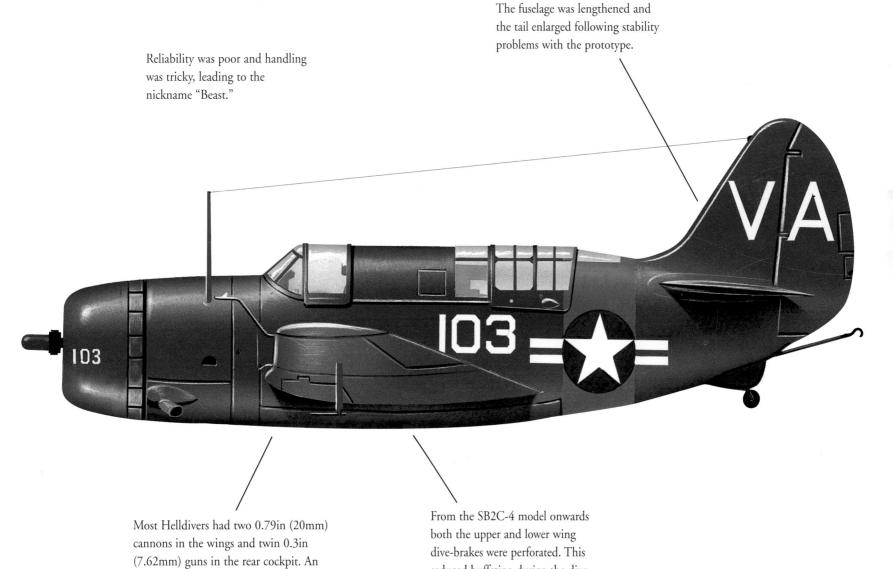

Most Helldivers had two 0.79in (20mm) cannons in the wings and twin 0.3in (7.62mm) guns in the rear cockpit. An internal bay could carry 2,000lb (907kg) of bombs or other stores.

From the SB2C-4 model onwards both the upper and lower wing dive-brakes were perforated. This reduced buffeting during the dive.

GRUMMAN XF10F JAGUAR *(1952)*

In 40 years of fighter development from the FF biplane to the F-14 Tomcat, the only Grumman fighters not accepted by the US Navy were the XF5F-1 Skyrocket and the XF10F-1 Jaguar.

Created as a redesigned F9F Panther in 1948, the Jaguar evolved into a tubby aircraft sporting the first variable geometry or "swing wings" to be used on any warplane. This, and its associated system of flaps and spoilers, proved far too complicated, but most of the trouble came from the tiny tailplane and the Jaguar proved almost impossible to keep in balanced flight.

Perhaps uniquely in the annals of naval aviation the cancellation effort was led by the Navy's project officer, usually the person most loyal to any project, whatever its faults. The flying Jaguar was used to test carrier deck crash barriers and the static test airframe became a target for tank guns.

SPECIFICATIONS

CREW:	1
ENGINE:	one 6,800lb (30.2kN) thrust Westinghouse XJ40-W-8 turbojet
MAX SPEED:	710mph (1,142km/h)
SPAN:	unswept spread 50ft 7in (15.48m); swept spread 36ft 8in (11.19m)
LENGTH:	54ft (16.46m)
HEIGHT:	16ft 3in (4.95m)
WEIGHT:	maximum 35,450lb (16,094kg)

Left: Resting on their laurels as the premier designer of US Navy fighters, Grumman achieved large orders for the Jaguar despite not having tested the swing-wing concept on a testbed. The Jaguar only made 32 flights, all of them eventful, before the program was terminated.

Unlike the variable-geometry wings on later fighters, where only the outer panel moved, the whole wing on the XF10F "translated," with a complex arrangement of moving panels to fill the gaps.

At maximum wing sweep the directional control was marginal, not helped by the ineffective rudder. The spoiler system was so complicated it was disconnected, leaving only tiny ailerons, which gave a very poor roll response.

At full sweep the wings were only 35 degrees and the performance gains were largely negated by the extra weight of the wing sweep mechanism.

The tailplane was operated by a novel arrangement where the pilot controlled a small delta-wing airfoil at the tip of the tail bullet. This in turn moved the main elevator. Unfortunately, a lag in the response between stick and surface usually resulted in a Pilot Induced Oscillation (PIO) and the Jaguar was virtually uncontrollable much of the time.

The Jaguar was another of those naval aircraft crippled by the Westinghouse J40 engine, which underwent its own development problems and never received the intended afterburner.

NORTHROP B-35/B-49 FLYING WINGS *(1946)*

Although the B-35 was ordered as early as 1941, it was obvious by 1944 that the flying-wing bomber was going to miss World War II and would then be obsolescent. In preparation for the next war, a jet-powered version was begun. The piston-engined XB-35 flew in June 1946, and the jet YB-49 in October 1947. The YB-35 initially had contra-rotating propellers, and had endless trouble with the gearboxes and unwanted yaw, much delaying the program. The YB-49 performed well, but during pullout tests the No. 2 aircraft tumbled backwards and the outer wings fell off. Edwards Air Force Base was named after the unfortunate test pilot.

All sorts of versions were planned for bombing, reconnaissance and electronic intelligence, but while about a dozen aircraft were under completion, the whole project was canceled and all were scrapped.

SPECIFICATIONS (XB-35)

CREW:	9
ENGINE:	four 3,000hp (2,238kW) Pratt & Whitney R-4360 radials
MAX SPEED:	391mph (629km/h)
SPAN:	172ft (52.42m)
LENGTH:	53ft 1in (16.32m)
HEIGHT:	20ft (6.16m)
WEIGHT:	180,000lb (81,647kg)

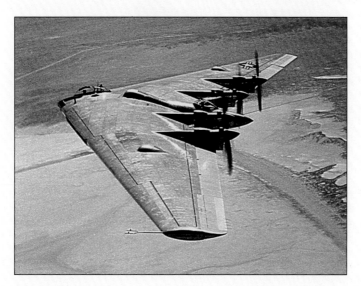

Left: The B-35 (pictured) and B-49 lost out to the more conventional Convair B-36, and the world had to wait until the 1990s for the first flying-wing bomber, the Northrop B-2, to enter service.

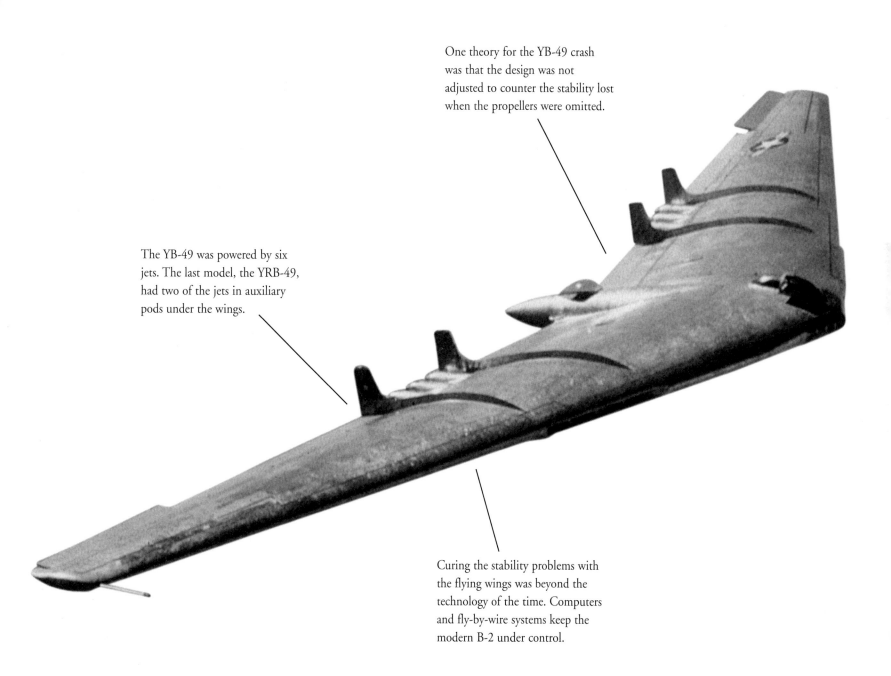

One theory for the YB-49 crash was that the design was not adjusted to counter the stability lost when the propellers were omitted.

The YB-49 was powered by six jets. The last model, the YRB-49, had two of the jets in auxiliary pods under the wings.

Curing the stability problems with the flying wings was beyond the technology of the time. Computers and fly-by-wire systems keep the modern B-2 under control.

NORTHROP XP-56 BLACK BULLET (1943)

For reasons that remain obscure, the Northrop XP-56 (first prototype natural metal, second olive drab) was nicknamed the "Black Bullet." It certainly resembled a bullet but lacked the projectile's speed or direction.

The first prototype had no vertical fin, and relied on its underfin more to protect the propeller than to provide stability. This arrangement, of course, was inadequate. Nose heaviness was corrected but became tail heaviness. During a fast taxi run the aircraft blew a tire, somersaulted and threw test pilot John Myers out. He was saved by his polo helmet and the second prototype was fitted with an upper fin. With a 2,000hp (1,492kW) engine, one thing the XP-56 was not was underpowered, but it proved slower than expected. The intended X-1800 water-cooled engine had been canceled and the substituted air-cooled radial was not the most suitable for a pusher layout. Fuel consumption was excessive and while waiting to conduct wind tunnel tests, the project was canceled.

SPECIFICATIONS

CREW:	1
ENGINE:	one 2,000hp (1,492kW) Pratt & Whitney R-2800-29 radial piston engine
MAX SPEED:	465mph (748km/h)
SPAN:	42ft 6in (12.95m)
LENGTH:	27ft 6in (8.38m)
HEIGHT:	11ft (3.35m)
WEIGHT:	maximum 12,145lb (5,509kg)

Left: In original form, the XP-56 was one of a long and diverse series of Northrop flying wings. Modifications to achieve stability made it a slightly more conventional aircraft, but not a viable fighter within the army's budget deadlines.

The planned armament was four
0.79in (20mm) cannons and four
0.5in (12.7mm) machine guns
in the nose, although this was
never fitted.

In a later modification the
ailerons were operated by bellows
fed by intakes in the wingtips.

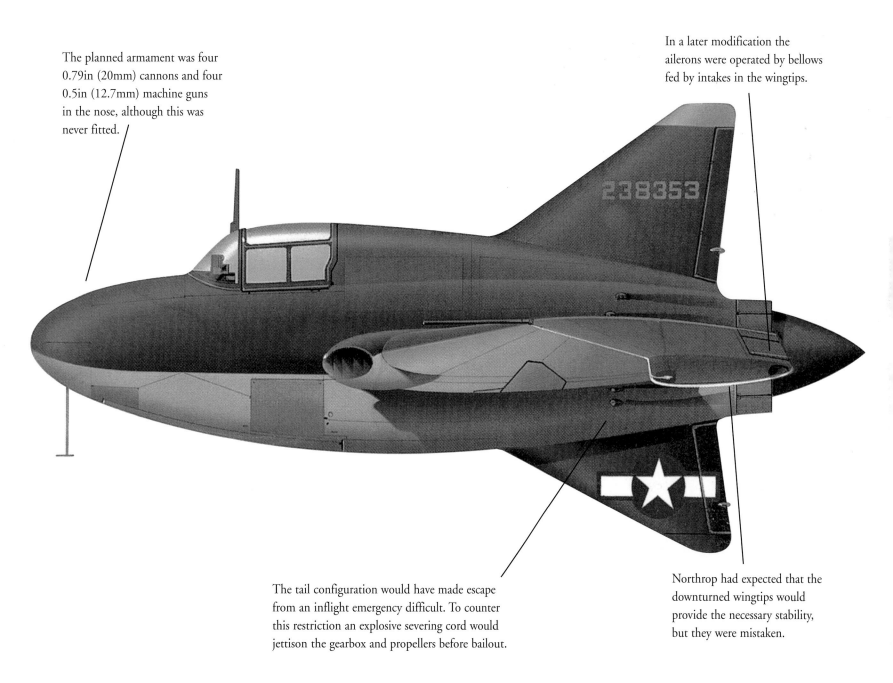

The tail configuration would have made escape
from an inflight emergency difficult. To counter
this restriction an explosive severing cord would
jettison the gearbox and propellers before bailout.

Northrop had expected that the
downturned wingtips would
provide the necessary stability,
but they were mistaken.

71

ROLLS-ROYCE "FLYING BEDSTEAD" *(1954)*

The very basic Thrust Measuring Rig or "Flying Bedstead" was the first British VTOL aircraft and gathered useful data for the P.1127 (Harrier) project. The Bedstead's loaded weight was only about 600lb (272kg) less than the combined thrust of the two engines, and some of that thrust was ducted away for the control ducts. Each control movement reduced the lifting thrust, requiring a bit more throttle and meaning that it could not be controlled at maximum thrust without a height loss. There was little margin for error – and none at all if one engine faltered. The only plus side was that the engine nozzles were arranged to give thrust (lift) on the centreline so that at least it would plunge vertically rather than flip over. Both Bedsteads did crash, one fatally, and the Harrier adopted a quite different lift system.

SPECIFICATIONS

CREW:	1
ENGINE:	two 4,050lb (18kN) thrust Rolls-Royce Nene turbojets
MAX SPEED:	n/a
LENGTH:	unknown
HEIGHT:	unknown
WEIGHT:	loaded 7,500lb (3,400kg)

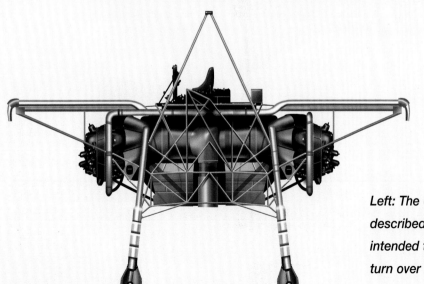

Left: The UK's first vertical takeoff aircraft, the Bedstead has been described as the most dangerous flying machine ever tested. Not intended to travel any distance, it had just 10 minutes' fuel and would turn over if landed with any forward speed.

The pilot's control stick opened and closed valves that directed compressed air to the nozzles mounted at front and rear and on the sides.

The pilot was totally exposed in his seat above the rig. Only after the initial test program was over was a rudimentary rollover cage added to offer some crash protection.

Like all early jet engines, the Nene took a while to spool up to a new power setting, meaning adjustments had to be made before they were needed.

Glossary

aerodynamic Having a shape that allows for low air resistance.

afterburner a mechanism at the end of a turbojet engine that helps it provide extra power.

airframe A plane not including the engines.

ft The abbreviation for the distance measurement foot.

i The abbreviation for inch.

km The abbreviation for the unit of length known as the kilometer.

m The abbreviation for meter.

Mach A calculation that represents the speed of an aircraft in relation to the speed of sound.

mph Also mi/h, an abbreviation that means miles per hour.

piston The cylindrical device in an engine that transfers power from the fuel combustion to the propellers.

posthumous A work that is completed after one dies.

propeller A bladed device that accelerates air to move a plane forward.

prototype An experimental model of a plane.

reconnaissance An exploratory mission to gather information.

squadron A military unit.

tail span The diameter of the tail of a plane.

VTO An abbreviation that stands for vertical takeoff.

wingspan The diameter of the wings of a plane from one end to the other.

For More Information

Aircraft Engine Historical Society, Inc.

1019 Old Monrovia Road NW, Suite 201

Huntsville, AL 35806

(256) 683-1458

Web site: http://www.enginehistory.org

A nonprofit historical society that celebrates the people and their ingenuity in the development and use of aircraft engines.

American Aviation Historical Society

2333 Otis Street

Santa Ana, CA 92704

(714) 549-4818

Web site: http://www.aahs-online.org

Since 1956 the American Aviation Historical Society has been preserving the rich heritage of American aviation. With a large collection of books, documents, and photographs, the organization provides information on interesting and often little-known facts associated with American aviation.

National Mall Building

Independence Ave at 6th Street, SW

Washington, DC 20560

Web site: http://www.nasm.si.edu

Part of the Smithsonian Institution, the Air and Space Museum chronicles the history of flight from the Wright brothers to present-day space explorations.

Planes of Fame

7000 Merrill Ave #17

Chino, CA 91710

(909) 597-3722

Web site: http://www.planesoffame.org

An independently operated, non-profit organization, Planes of Fame is an aviation museum that is dedicated to preserving aircraft and their memories for educational benefit.

Society for Aviation History

P.O. Box 7081

San Carlos, CA 94070

(650) 631-4207

Web site: http://www.sfahistory.org

The Society for Aviation History was formed as a part of the American Aviation Historical Society in 1985. It is dedicated to preserving the past, present, and future aviation history.

WEB SITES

Due to the changing nature of Internet links, Rosen Publishing has developed an online list of Web sites related to the subject of this book. This site is updated regularly. Please use this link to access the list:

http://www.rosenlinks.com/wwid/woai

For Further Reading

Caoimh, Fia O. *The Aviation Book: A Survey of the World's Aircraft*. San Francisco, CA: Chronicle Books, 2006.

Grant, R. G. *Flight*. New York, NY: DK Publishing, Inc., 2007.

Green, William, and Gordon Swanborough. *Illustrated Anatomy of the World's Fighters*. Osceola, WI: Zenith Press, 2001.

Gunston, Bill. *Aviation: The First 100 Years*. Hauppauge, NY: Barron's Educational Series, 2002.

Heppenheimer, T. A. *Flight: A History of Aviation in Photographs*. New York, NY: Firefly Books, 2004.

Jarrett, Philip. *Ultimate Aircraft*. New York, NY: DK Publishing, Inc., 2000.

Milstein, Jeffrey. *AirCraft: The Jet as Art*. New York, NY: Harry N. Abrams, Inc., 2007.

Newhouse, John. *Boeing versus Airbus: The Inside Story of the Greatest International Competition in Business*. New York, NY: Vintage, 2008.

Patterson, Dan. *50 Aircraft that Changed the World*. Ontario, Canada: Boston Mills Press, 2007.

Winchester, Jim. *The Encyclopedia of Modern Aircraft: From Civilian Airliners to Military Superfighters*. New York, NY: Thunder Bay Press, 2006.

Index

DATE DUE
